Reaffirming Life in a Culture of Death

A Catholic Response to Critical Issues

Mark Neilsen

LIGUORI
PUBLICATIONS

One Liguori Drive
Liguori, MO 63057-9999
(314) 464-2500

Imprimi Potest:
James Shea, C.SS.R.
Provincial, St. Louis Province
The Redemptorists

Imprimatur:
+ Paul Zipfel, V.G.
Auxiliary Bishop, Archdiocese of St. Louis

ISBN 0-89243-871-1
Library of Congress Catalog Card Number: 95-80149
Copyright © 1996, Mark Neilsen

This book is a revised and updated edition of *8 Key Issues in Modern Society: A Catholic Perspective,* © 1990, Liguori Publications.

Printed in the United States of America
3 5 7 9 8 6 4 2
Cover design by Grady Gunter
Cover photo by Tony Stone Images

To my wife, Judy,
with love and gratitude.

CONTENTS

———

INTRODUCTION

———

The social mission of the Catholic Church has received un-precedented attention over the past two decades, thanks in great measure to *The Challenge of Peace: God's Promise and Our Response,* the U.S. Catholic bishops' 1983 pastoral letter on war and peace. At a time when policymakers were discussing how to survive an approaching nuclear "Armageddon," this document was read and discussed—though not always heeded—at the highest levels of our government and in the news media.

Within the universal Church and on an international scale, the speeches and writings of Pope John Paul II, especially those on labor and social development, have given a tremendous spur to Catholic social doctrine. As he has traveled around the globe, he has again and again addressed social issues and defended the dignity of the human person. But his most lasting contribu-tion will surely be his many written statements and encyclicals on Catholic social doctrine, which have drawn the attention of policymakers and scholars alike.

But while many rejoice that Catholic social thought has

gained this spotlight, others regard this development fearfully, as a dangerous mix of politics and religion, a blend that does more harm than good. Some even go so far as to argue that a rising interest in worldly affairs among Catholics signals a decline of their belief in humanity's supernatural destiny. In actuality, Catholic social teaching is deeply rooted in the scriptural account of creation and in the Church's traditional mission to care for the poor.

Just as the Old Testament prophets called Israel to practice justice and to be faithful to its covenant with Yahweh, so Jesus in the gospels reminds us of our obligation to the poor. No more clearly does he spell this out than in his parable of the Last Judgment in Matthew's Gospel. The king welcomes the faithful, saying, "Truly I tell you, just as you did it to one of the least of these who are members of my family, you did it to me" (Matthew 25:40). In John's Gospel, Jesus declares, "This is my commandment, that you love one another as I have loved you" (John 15:12).

From its beginnings, the Church has sought to understand and live out this command. Just as the practice of charity and the defense of the weak mark the lives of some of our greatest saints, active social ministry has been a necessary task of the Church. Early leaders like Augustine wrote at length about the Christian's duties to society. Having come to accept faith in Jesus Christ, people have always asked, "How ought we now to live?" Thomas Aquinas and other theologians posed the question in philosophical terms that continue to frame Church teachings today. Because this philosophical tradition places a high value on precision and painstaking reasoning, papal encyclicals and bishops' pastoral letters are sometimes difficult for many Catholics to understand.

Nevertheless, Catholic social teaching is not something simply "added on" to the Good News of Jesus Christ. In the words of Pope John Paul II, the Church's social doctrine is "an essential part of the Christian message, since this doctrine points out the direct consequences of that message in the life of society and situates daily work and the struggles for justice in the context of bearing witness to Christ the Savior" (*On the Hundredth Anniversary*, #5).

One of the purposes of this book is to look at what the Church has to say about some of today's key social issues. Those who look in these pages for pat answers to complex social problems or a blueprint for living will be disappointed. Catholic social thought is neither a political treatise nor a list of *do*'s and *don't*'s. What this book does provide is a set of guidelines for Christian decision-making and for help in evaluating social changes and policies that affect human development. Reading the signs of the times, the Church has sought to bring about a more just social order by appealing to humanity's best instincts.

Sources of Social Doctrine

The modern era of Catholic social thought began with Pope Leo XIII's encyclical letter *On the Condition of Workers* (*Rerum Novarum*, 1891). Responding to the great changes in European society brought about by industrialization and urbanization, Pope Leo wrote his letter as a plea for an end to the exploitation of working people. He called for a just and living wage and for the right of workers to form unions and bargain collectively. Considered a radical by some critics, Pope Leo nevertheless made it quite clear that Catholic tradition supported the right to private property and to a fair profit.

The social message of the Church has become more prominent in the past thirty years as a result of important social encyclicals by three of the last four popes. In addition, one of the major documents of Vatican II, the *Pastoral Constitution on the Church in the Modern World,* addressed key social issues. This document had a tremendous effect on the Church because it presented a teaching on social doctrine by all the world's bishops speaking together with the pope in an ecumenical council. All of these documents have propelled the Church into greater dialogue with the secular world on social issues.

Through this dialogue has developed what Cardinal Joseph Bernardin of Chicago has termed "a consistent ethic of life": the philosophy of defending the dignity of human life from conception through infancy, childhood, and adulthood, and on to the very brink of death.

Human Dignity in Society

All Catholic social teaching grows out of the conviction that each one of us has inalienable value because we have been made in God's own image. No human law or institution confers this value, and no human law or institution can take it away. Formed out of love, we are the summit of all creation and are destined to spend eternity with God. The human person is, therefore, entitled to the highest respect and care. Thus, the essential dignity of the human person is the first pillar of Catholic social teaching.

The second pillar is humanity's social nature. From the moment of conception, we rely on others. First in the family and later as a member of the national and world community, each of us depends on others not only for our physical well-being but for our moral, intellectual, and spiritual development as well.

A culture like ours often overlooks humanity's social dimension, so devoted are we to the "virtue" of rugged individualism. But just as an infant relies on others for food, so each of us needs a society in which to learn and develop our full potential as human beings. Christians, moreover, need a community of faith to help us worship and grow closer to God. Because of this social dimension, the well-being of society itself is necessarily a concern for the Church.

Absolute Principles and Conditional Judgments

While some observers have criticized Catholic social teaching for going too far in tackling social issues, others have been frustrated that it hasn't gone far enough in suggesting viable alternatives. Although the Church insists that Christians must exercise a social responsibility, only rarely does it spell out what we should or should not do with our lives. Why? Like personal morality, social morality consists of principles that are put into practice through choices and actions. Because specific conditions change, the Church does not require the faithful to obey the practical or prudential judgments of Church leaders. All Catholics, however, are expected to give serious consideration to the principles of Catholic social teaching as well as the prudential judgments of the bishops and the popes.

An example of the difference between absolute principles and prudential judgments may be seen in the controversy over abortion legislation. Catholic teaching forbids the intentional killing of an unborn baby. This is an absolute principle. Some Church leaders argue that, based upon our legal system and today's social climate, Catholics ought to support a human-life amendment to the U.S. Constitution. That is a prudential judgment. Catholics may disagree with such a judgment, but we need to give it serious consideration because we will be called upon to vote and shoulder our responsibility for public-policy choices that protect life.

Catholics in the United States are uniquely positioned to respond to the Church's social teaching, citizens as we are of the most powerful and materially prosperous country in the world. We have the twin heritages of democratic traditions and a domestic Church with a history of civic involvement. In many areas, Church teaching and our national values are in alignment, as, for example, on the matter of freedom of religious assembly. Where there is not such a meeting of traditions, Church teaching challenges us to look at our national power, wealth, and political freedoms and to use them for the good of all people.

An "Option for the Poor"

Being critical of our own society or looking honestly at our own choices can be a difficult challenge, but it is not without its rewards. The recently coined term "preferential option for the poor" calls us to care especially about what happens to the poor and powerless among us, but this is not intended to pit one group against another. Rather, to serve God, Christians should pay attention to the weakest among us. The result of that service is not just that our community will grow stronger and more cohesive (and it will), but that we will grow closer to God and to one another.

In the final analysis, social issues matter to the Church because humanity, especially the poor, reveal something of God to all of us. Therefore, we hear the teachings of the Church and respond through action, not just to be in step with some new ecclesiastical vogue, but to experience God in the richness of our world, filled with its new problems and ever-changing challenges.

CHAPTER 1

ABORTION AND THE "LIFE ISSUES"

———

Of all the Catholic social teachings, the Roman Catholic Church's stance on abortion is the best known in the United States. Since the 1973 Supreme Court decision legalizing abortion on demand, the U.S. Catholic hierarchy and laity have fought energetically to overturn the ruling. On no other issue has the Church so consistently and vocally challenged prevailing social values. Indeed, this very energy has led some to criticize the Church for being a "single-issue" organization.

The U.S. Catholic bishops see opposition to abortion as a basic part of a "consistent ethic of life" that defends human life at all stages. In their 1985 statement *Pastoral Plan for Pro-Life Activities: A Reaffirmation,* they made the connection between the right to life and all other rights: "Basic human rights are violated in many ways: by abortion and euthanasia, by injustice and the denial of equality to individuals or various groups of persons, by some forms of human experimentation, by neglect of the underprivileged and disadvantaged who deserve society's concern and support" (#7).

Of course, abortion is the problem that it is today not simply because of a Supreme Court decision. Indeed, Pope John Paul II regards legal abortion as a symptom of a "profound crisis of culture" (*Gospel of Life*, #11). Many factors have lead to this crisis, including a deep contemporary skepticism about the roots of knowledge and ethical behavior; social systems that increasingly isolate individuals and families to face problems on their own; and the cycle of poverty-frustration-violence, particularly against women, that leads people to desperate decisions.

The result is a culture that denies solidarity and in many cases takes the form of a veritable "culture of death," wrote the pope. "This culture is actively fostered by powerful cultural, economic and political currents which encourage an idea of society excessively concerned with efficiency" (*Gospel of Life*, #12).

The pope has called upon the Church to promote a "culture of life," rooted in the understanding that all life is a gift from God, and with that gift comes responsibility. In addition to legislative changes, years of education and action will be necessary to provide a more supportive environment for human life in our world.

This means that opposition to abortion requires legislative and social changes that not only safeguard the right to life but also make it easier for families and individuals to welcome a new life. Recognizing the difficulties women and men face in society, the Church seeks always to defend the right to life as the fundamental human right.

The First Step of a Wider Campaign

The campaign against abortion is really the first stage of a wider campaign in defense of the human person. This campaign essentially began with the promulgation in 1974 of *Declaration on Abortion* by the Vatican Sacred Congregation for the Doctrine of the Faith.

Although there can be many different views on the morality of an issue like abortion in a pluralistic society, the Vatican's position is that "one can never claim freedom of opinion as a pretext for attacking the rights of others, most especially the right to life" (*Declaration on Abortion*, #2). The document asserts that during pregnancy the child's right to life takes precedence over the mother's freedom of choice. This distinction is worth noting: it is not that the mother has no rights; rather, there is a conflict of rights that, says the Church, must be resolved in the child's favor.

Although the debate surrounding abortion has intensified dramatically since 1973, the Church's position has ancient roots. The *Declaration on Abortion* cites an unbroken Catholic opposition to the practice since its earliest days. In the *Didache*, the early Church's collection of teachings believed to have come directly from the apostles, it is written, "You shall not kill by abortion the fruit of the womb and you shall not murder the infant already born" (#6). And during the Middle Ages, abortion was always treated as a grave sin.

The right to life is fundamentally human, regardless of the person's stage of development. The *Declaration on Abortion* puts it simply: "Any discrimination based on the various stages of life is no more justified than any other discrimination. The right to life remains complete in an old person, even one greatly weakened; it is not lost by one who is incurably sick. The right to life is no less to be respected in the small infant just born than in the mature person. In reality, respect for human life is called for from the time that the process of generation begins. From the time that the ovum is fertilized, a life is begun which is neither that of the father nor of the mother, it is rather the life of a new human being with his [or her] own growth. It would never be made human if it were not human already" (#12).

Just how seriously the Church takes this position may be seen in the Vatican document *In the Service of Life*, issued by the Pontifical Council for the Family in 1992. This document urges doctors to inform their patients and the general public that contraceptives such as IUDs (intrauterine devices) and some chemical compounds actually abort a fertilized ovum. Whether the abortion is caused by chemicals or mechanical instruments, it represents the same decision to terminate human life.

The right to life, like all other human rights, is our birthright as daughters and sons of God; the state does not confer it, nor can the state withdraw it. The state is, however, obliged to protect human life through civil law, according to Church teaching.

The Church does not assert that civil law need be the equivalent of moral law, for practical reasons as well as reasons of fairness to the rights of others. But the right to life is seen as so basic and so essential that it is necessary to make abortion a crime, for the same reasons that virtually all civilized societies regard murder as criminal.

Because the Catholic Church in the United States seeks to use the law to defend the right to life, some people have argued that this amounts to imposing religious beliefs on those of differing faiths. *In the Service of Life* responds to this criticism, "It is true that it is not the task of the law to choose between points of view or to impose one rather than another. But the life of the child takes precedence over all opinions. One cannot invoke freedom of thought to destroy this life" (#20).

In *The Gospel of Life,* Pope John Paul II explained the danger of using individual freedom to justify the permissibility of abortion. "Freedom negates and destroys itself, and becomes a factor leading to the destruction of others, when it no longer recognizes and respects its *essential link with the truth*" (#19). If individual freedom and autonomy become absolute values, "some kind of compromise must be found, if one wants a society in which the maximum possible freedom is guaranteed to each individual. In this way, any reference to common values and to a truth absolutely binding on everyone is lost, and social life ventures on to the shifting sands of complete relativism. At that point, *everything is negotiable, everything is open to bargaining:* even the first of the fundamental rights, the right to life" (#20).

Once abortion is made legal, practical consequences follow. The Vatican's *Declaration on Abortion* warns that removing the punishment from the act of abortion gives the impression that it is now a legitimate option. It seems beyond question that in the United States abortion has increasingly been used as a means of birth control since the 1973 Supreme Court decision. Although judges and legislators often say they regard abortion as evil, in refusing to outlaw it, they are creating a situation in which an evil grows more and more commonplace.

In response, the Church believes that abortion should not be a legal option and that Catholics are not bound to obey any law that would "admit in principle the liceity [permissibility] of abortion. Nor can he [or she] take part in a propaganda campaign in favor of such a law, or vote for it. Moreover, he [or she] may not collaborate in its application" (#22).

The Church's position remains firm even in the cases of rape, incest, or danger to the health of the mother. In cases of rape or incest, the Church argues that no good will be done by making the unborn child the second victim of a tragedy. When a mother's life is actually endangered by pregnancy, the Church recognizes a conflict but maintains that the unborn child cannot be directly and intentionally killed.

Up to this point, it might seem that the Catholic position on abortion cannot be said to be truly "pro-life" since it seems simply opposed to abortion. But the Church recognizes that abortion is very often a heart-wrenching last resort to extremely difficult circumstances and supports legislation and action to aid those who are faced with desperate social and economic pressures to choose abortion.

Social Supports

The *Declaration on Abortion* outlines some of the social supports that can ease the burden a new life can bring to a family: "Help for families and for unmarried mothers, assured grants for children, a statute for illegitimate [*sic*] children and reasonable arrangements for adoption—a whole positive policy must be put into force so that there will always be a concrete, honorable and positive alternative to abortion" (#23).

In reality, the Church's position against abortion is a call for human rights and for a society in which human dignity might better be maintained. "One can never approve of abortion; but it is above all necessary to combat its causes" (#26). In the United States, whether or not the political and legal battle to end abortion is ever successful, the Church challenges us to go further to develop a consistent ethic of life for all people.

One obvious need in our country is for adequate healthcare for low-income pregnant women and newborn children. Poor mothers need adequate financial support so they can stay home with their preschool children and quality childcare so they can work when their children are old enough. As individuals and as a society, we are obligated, the Church teaches, to provide alternatives to abortion, especially for the poor.

Sexual responsibility is another area in which there is much to be done, particularly by and for men. Abortion is generally considered a women's issue. Far too often, if the man who fathered the child enters the discussion at all, it is to encourage the woman to abort the child. Men fail to take responsibility for their children at an alarming rate in our society, and this tendency must change if abortion is to be rejected as an alternative. Men must figure into any discussion of abortion and its aftermath, just as they ought to assume financial and other paternal obligations toward their children.

A Culture of Death

When a nation or culture accepts abortion as a legitimate choice, it does more than simply accept a surgical procedure; it fosters a climate of opinion in which human life can be eliminated with impunity. Describing the evil of abortion as "an avalanche sweeping away even those who are not fully aware of it," *In the Service of Life* argues that the prevalence of abortion has direct effects across the board on a society's scientific, cultural, and political life.

To undermine support for the inviolability of human life, a variety of arguments are put forth to justify laws permitting abortion. "This phenomenon would not have been possible without the cooperation, or at least the failure to act, of some scientists, jurists, moralists and even theologians. In the name of pluralism, of the numerical majority and of respect for opinions, the dignity of the person is in fact trampled under foot" *(In the Service of Life)*.

To stem the advance of the abortion mentality, a renewed appreciation for the dignity of the human person needs to be fostered in society through authentic scientific research, renewed cultural life—especially in the family—and political action on the local, national, and even international scene.

The U.S. Catholic bishops see a connection between the acceptance of abortion and the increase in violence throughout our society. "We are tragically turning to violence in the search for quick and easy answers to complex human problems," wrote the bishops in *Confronting a Culture of Violence* (1994). "A society which destroys its children, abandons its old, and relies on vengeance fails fundamental moral tests. Violence is not the solution; it is the most clear sign of our failures."

The U.S. bishops also made it clear that violence has no place in the struggle against abortion: "For our part, we oppose both the violence of abortion and the use of violence to oppose abortion. We are clear in our total repudiation of any effort to advocate or carry out murder in the name of the pro-life cause. Such acts cannot be justified" *(Confronting a Culture of Violence)*.

Whether or not we can reduce or prohibit abortions through changes in the law, all Catholics will have to be part of the continuing struggle to make a place in our nation for all children, even the most "unwanted," if our faith is to be truly pro-life.

Euthanasia

The Church defines "mercy killing," or euthanasia, as "an action or an omission which of itself or by intention causes death in order to save a person from suffering or relieve the family or society from the burden of caring for the individual" *(Declaration on Euthanasia, p. 8).*

The Sacred Congregation issued *Declaration on Euthanasia* because changes in medical technologies as well as in our conception of death have made it unclear where the responsibility to administer care ends and euthanasia begins. At the same time, contemporary society, according to Pope John Paul II, is characterized by "a cultural climate which fails to perceive any meaning or value in suffering, but rather considers suffering the epitome of evil, to be eliminated at all costs. This is especially the case in the absence of a religious outlook which could help to provide a positive understanding of the mystery of suffering" (*Gospel of Life,* #15).

Human suffering, so often a crucial part of the discussion of euthanasia, has special significance for Christians. "According to Christian teaching, suffering, especially during the last moments of life, has a special place in God's saving plan; it is in fact a sharing in Christ's passion and a union with the redeeming sacrifice which He offered in obedience with the Father's will" (*Declaration on Euthanasia,* p. 13).

Accepted in this spirit, suffering is never "pointless." But the Church recognizes that such acceptance is heroic and cannot be demanded of an individual. Church teaching allows, therefore, the use of painkilling drugs, provided their purpose is not to hasten death or intentionally cause unconsciousness. The approach of death is considered an opportunity for a person to prepare for meeting the Creator and for taking leave of his or her family.

The Church's teaching on euthanasia allows for compassionate and humane care of the sick yet accepts the inevitability of death. "Life is a gift of God," says the *Declaration on Euthanasia,* "and on the other hand death is unavoidable; it is necessary, therefore, that we without in any way hastening the hour of death, should be able to accept it with full responsibility and dignity" (p. 156). The challenge is to accept death but not to cause it in our desire to escape pain.

Why does the Church make such an issue of pain when it appears so obviously humane to put a terminally ill patient out of his or her misery? One reason is that human suffering comes in all shapes and sizes and in all stages of life. If it is permissible to avoid suffering toward the end of life, then the next question is, why should anyone endure great suffering at all?

The whole range of human suffering has received the attention of Pope John Paul II in an apostolic letter. The pope sees suffering as a mystery of the human condition and "an invitation to manifest the moral greatness of man" (*Christian Meaning of Human Suffering*, #22). Even the dying may display that greatness: "When this body is gravely ill, totally incapacitated, and the person is almost incapable of living and acting, all the more do interior maturity and spiritual greatness become evident, constituting a touching lesson to those who are healthy and normal" (#26).

The Church's teaching on euthanasia is meant to assist those who must make difficult decisions at the time of grave illness. The Vatican document states that while everyone has the duty to take care of his or her health, "extraordinary means" to sustain life need not necessarily be taken. Advances in medical technology have made commonplace procedures that used to be considered extraordinary, and the Vatican speaks of "proportionate" and "disproportionate" means of treatment and asks, will the good of the result outweigh the bad of the treatment?

The *Declaration on Euthanasia* states that "it will be possible to make a correct judgment as to the means by studying the type of treatment to be used, its degree of complexity or risk, its cost and the possibilities of using it, and comparing these elements with the result that can be expected, taking into account the state of the sick person and his or her physical and moral resources" (p. 11). Clearly, Church teaching does not answer every question of medical treatment for the dying, but it suggests that the very process of making the decision is important and should be the province, not of documents or legislated absolutes, but of consultation between the sick person and his or her family and medical caregivers.

To safeguard the rights of the sick and dying, the U.S. bishops' Committee on Pro-Life Activities in 1984 wrote *Guidelines for Legislation on Life-Sustaining Treatment,* in which they urge that legislation always presuppose the right of an individual to life and to the medical care necessary to sustain life. The right to refuse medical treatment, said the bishops, should be seen as a corollary to the right to request it. Because the decision to withhold or give treatment is so complex, it is a mistake to give too much power to proxy decisions or to a document, like a "living will," that cannot take into full account the specifics of a situation.

In addition to the theological opposition to euthanasia, there are sociological reasons to resist contemporary "right to die" or "rational suicide" movements. Just as abortion is offered as a solution to the economic burdens pregnant low-income mothers face, so too is euthanasia one obvious solution to the great costs of healthcare, especially for the country's elderly population.

The average age of the U.S. population will increase over the next several decades, and more and more elderly will require costly medical care. At the other end of the continuum, more and more elaborate and expensive technologies are being developed for infants with medical problems. Added to these factors, the long-range effects upon healthcare of the AIDS epidemic can scarcely be estimated. The "right to die" movement may in the coming years gain adherents not only among those who never want to suffer, but also among those who must pay the medical bills.

Conclusion

As Pope John Paul II has so eloquently warned the modern world, "powerful cultural, economic and political currents" tend to cast these life-and-death issues in terms of pragmatism and efficiency. "Looking at the situation from this point of view, it is possible to speak in a certain sense of a *war of the powerful against the weak:* a life which would require greater acceptance, love and care is considered useless, or held to be an intolerable burden, and is therefore rejected in one way or another. A person who, because of illness, handicap or, more simply, just by existing, compromises the well-being or lifestyle of those who are more favored tends to be looked upon as an enemy to be resisted or eliminated. In this way a kind of *'conspiracy against life'* is unleashed" (*Gospel of Life,* #12).

Catholic social teaching opposes this "conspiracy against life." Each human being must be accorded due respect as a son or daughter of God, from the earliest moments of human existence until the last. Society has an obligation, according to Church teaching, to protect our right to be born as well as to experience in all its fullness the mystery of death.

For Further Discussion

1. In their *Pastoral Plan for Pro-Life Activities: A Reaffirmation,* the U.S. Catholic bishops said that "society's responsibility to ensure and protect human rights demands recognition and protection of the right to life as antecedent to all other rights and the necessary condition for their realization. It is

unlikely that efforts to protect other rights will ultimately be successful if life itself is continually diminished in value" (#7). Should Catholics make political decisions, like voting for a candidate, on the basis of the single issue of abortion?

2. If abortion were made illegal, what would happen? How would the law be enforced? And how would the Church be called to respond by its "consistent ethic of life"?

3. If abortion remains legal and if governmental aid for impoverished mothers is reduced, will that increase the pressure on a poor woman to have an abortion? Put another way, what social conditions and governmental policies can encourage the formation of families capable of caring for their children?

4. What kind of support can Catholics and Church institutions give to those with life-threatening or terminal illnesses? What kind of care would you want if your medical condition was considered terminal?

CHAPTER 2

CAPITAL PUNISHMENT

———

A seventeen-year-old girl is abducted by two men as she leaves her job at a filling station, then raped and strangled. Her body is later found dumped in a field. The two men responsible are soon apprehended and eventually found guilty of having committed this horrible crime on a destructive and vicious whim. What should their punishment be?

Without a doubt, some kind of punishment for criminals is essential—violent crime inflicts too great a toll on our society to let it proceed without penalty. Deeds that are scarcely imaginable have become commonplace items on the late-night news, and the resulting fear undermines any sense of community. Everyone agrees something must be done—but what?

Capital punishment, a key issue during the 1988 presidential campaign, stirs up a welter of emotions. The helplessness, vulnerability, revulsion, and just plain anger we feel in the face of a truly heinous act—mass murder, terrorist bombing, torture—is so difficult to bear that we desperately seek immediate justice. Capital punishment has the look of being a solution, a dramatic and final act to demonstrate society's willingness to "do something."

But capital punishment is not just a symbol; it is the taking of human life by the state and as such has implications for society that may be harmful. If such a punishment makes our society more brutal, with even less compassion toward our fellow human beings and less reverence for life itself, then it will not make our streets any safer.

The U.S. Catholic bishops, as well as Pope John Paul II, have asked Catholics and public policymakers to reconsider whether or not capital punishment makes sense in today's world. At the foundation of their position is the conviction that *"not even a murderer loses his* [or her] *personal dignity"* (*Gospel of Life*, #9). They neither underestimate the problem of crime nor deny the right of a community to protect itself. Rather, they urge us to explore an approach to crime and punishment that is at once both realistic and compassionate.

Punishment in the Old and New Laws

"An eye for an eye and a tooth for a tooth," the Hebrew law of punishment, brings a certain symmetry and satisfaction to our dealings with those who injure us. Though the formula may seem crude to us, it was actually considered a moderate approach to punishment in a culture in which revenge was often brutal and capricious violence toward women and slaves was commonplace. In the Old Testament books of Exodus and Leviticus, capital punishment was to be applied to specific crimes.

Jesus, however, revealed a new law: "'You have heard that it was said, "An eye for an eye and a tooth for a tooth." But I say to you, Do not resist an evildoer. But if anyone strikes you on the right cheek, turn the other also...'" (Matthew 5:38–39). Later in the gospel story, "Peter came and said to him, 'Lord, if another member of the church sins against me, how often should I forgive? As many as seven times?' Jesus said to him, 'Not seven times, but, I tell you, seventy-seven times'" (Matthew 18:21–22). Jesus then made it clear through a parable that his followers must forgive their brothers and sisters "from their hearts."

Since Jesus not only preached forgiveness and forbearance toward those who injure us but was himself wrongfully condemned to death, it may be surprising to learn that Church tradition has supported the death penalty. Thomas Aquinas justified capital punishment when the common good of the society or the stability of the state was at risk.

While Catholic teaching supports the right of the state to protect its citizens and institutions, "the question for judgment and decision today," said the U.S. Catholic bishops in their 1980 statement on capital punishment, "is whether capital punishment is justifiable under present circumstances" (*Statement on Capital Punishment*, #4).

Pope John Paul II similarly has supported society's right to protect itself and defend public order, but he has opposed the use of the death penalty "except in cases of absolute necessity: in other words, when it would not be possible otherwise to defend society. Today, however, as a result of steady improvements in the organization of the penal system, such cases are very rare, if not practically non-existent" (*Gospel of Life*, #56).

The pope went on to cite the *Catechism of the Catholic Church*: "If bloodless means are sufficient to defend human lives against an aggressor and to protect public order and the safety of persons, public authority must limit itself to such means, because they better correspond to the concrete conditions of the common good and are more in conformity to the dignity of the human person" (*Catechism*, #2267). With this statement in mind, we can more fully appreciate the U.S. bishops' position on criminal justice.

The Purpose of Punishment

The bishops pointed out that three justifications are usually given for any kind of punishment: retribution, deterrence, and reform. Can these justifications, they asked, be applied to capital punishment, the most extreme form of punishment?

Reform cannot be used as justification because capital punishment deprives the criminal of the opportunity to develop a new way of life. Deterrence is a more complex question. At the least, capital punishment prevents the criminal from committing additional crimes. But the available evidence is inconclusive about the deterrent effects of executing the relatively few criminals who are on death row. There are approximately two thousand of them, and ten times that number of murders are committed each year in the United States. According to criminologists, most offenders don't believe they will be caught when they commit a crime, and few seem to consider the punishment that might await them. The U.S. bishops put it this way: "There are strong reasons to doubt that many crimes of violence are undertaken in a spirit of rational calculation which would be influenced by a remote threat of death" (*Statement on Capital Punishment*, #6). Besides, even at its swiftest imposition, capital punishment necessarily comes after a lengthy and complex legal process that often serves to disconnect the punishment from the offense, and this only decreases any deterrent effect capital punishment might have.

Granting that the need for retribution does justify punishment, the bishops argue that it does not require or justify the taking of the criminal's life. While it would be wrong and damaging to society for a criminal to go unpunished, it would be just as wrong to inflict too harsh a punishment. "Thus we would regard it as barbarous and inhumane for a criminal who had tortured or maimed a victim to be tortured or maimed in return. Such a punishment might satisfy certain vindictive desires that we or the victim might feel, but the satisfaction of such desires is not and cannot be an objective of a humane and Christian approach to punishment" (*Statement on Capital Punishment*, #8).

A desire for revenge is evident among some supporters of the death penalty. When convicted mass murderer Theodore Bundy was executed in Florida in early 1989, a carnival atmosphere prevailed outside the prison on the night of his death. Cheers greeted the announcement that the sentence had been carried out, and several people in the crowd said they wished his punishment could have been worse. Without in any way condoning or making excuses for the kind of crimes Bundy perpetrated, Catholic teaching never validates revenge as a motive for the death penalty.

The U.S. bishops believe that there would be definite social benefits to abolishing capital punishment. In the first place, its abolition would signal our willingness to end the cycle of violence and find alternative ways of dealing with those who injure us. Second, it would demonstrate "our belief in the unique worth and dignity of each person from the moment of conception, a creature made in the image and likeness of God" (*Statement on Capital Punishment*, #11). The bishops believe it is particularly important in our day to affirm the dignity even of society's most "unwanted."

Third, the abolition of the death penalty would be a sign of our respect for human life at all stages. "We do not wish to equate the situation of criminals convicted of capital offenses with the condition of the innocent unborn or of the defenseless aged or infirm," the bishops cautioned, "but we do believe that the defense of life is strengthened by eliminating exercise of a judicial authorization to take human life" (*Statement on Capital Punishment*, #12).

Finally, the bishops noted that by abolishing the death penalty, we would more closely be following the example of Jesus, "who both taught and practiced the forgiveness of injustice and who came 'to give his life as a ransom for many' (Mk 10:45)" (*Statement on Capital Punishment*, #13). At the root of the bishops' call for the abolition of capital punishment is, even more than humane or philosophical considerations, their understanding of the life and message of Jesus Christ.

As Jesuit theologian John Langan has pointed out, "The case against capital punishment does not depend on our taking the view that the criminal is a victim of injustice or is a well-intentioned but misguided person who is now in trouble with the law. It turns on our seeing in him or her another human being made in God's image, fallible, sinful, in need of both support and conversion" ("Capital Punishment in America Today").

Forgiveness of one's enemies cannot be accomplished without God's grace. It is very difficult to love as Christ would a person who has injured us, especially if the injury was great. It is extremely difficult to see God's face in the face of the mass murderer or the terrorist, but our faith tells us it is there, even in the very least of our brothers and sisters. If we find this challenging, it is no less than the challenge of the gospel itself. With God's help, we can find the compassion we need.

Pope John Paul II has shown the world that he is personally willing to try to live up to the gospel standard of love for one's enemies. He offered a significant example of Christian forgiveness when he met with and forgave the man who had tried to assassinate him. On several occasions, the pope has pleaded for clemency for those about to be executed.

In addition to their desire to foster positive social values, the U.S. bishops also want to do away with the death penalty to avoid certain problems inherent in the application of capital punishment. An obvious problem is that no matter how good the appeals process, the possibility of executing an innocent person always exists. Also, those various persons who actually commit capital crimes and are found guilty do not get identical treatment, for a variety of reasons, not the least of which is their ability to hire a good lawyer. Amnesty International, a human-rights group that opposes all forms of capital punishment as "cruel and unusual," concluded in 1987 that the death sentence is unequally applied in the United States in the thirty-seven states that permit it.

Furthermore, statistics show that those sentenced to die are usually poor and disproportionately black. "Abolition of the death penalty will not eliminate racism and its effects, an evil which we are called on to combat in many different ways," wrote the bishops. "But it is a reasonable judgment that racist attitudes and the social consequences of racism have some influence in determining who is sentenced to die in our society. This we do not regard as acceptable" (*Statement on Capital Punishment*, #19).

No Easy Answer

The bishops have candidly acknowledged that ending the death penalty would not solve the problems of crime and violence. They are aware of the great suffering that violent crimes bring to victims and their families, and they call upon our society and Church to offer the support these suffering ones need to put their lives back together. At the same time, the bishops have urged a restructuring of the criminal-justice system so that it is better able to rehabilitate offenders.

Their call to end the death penalty is also a plea for comprehensive social reform: "We acknowledge that there is a pressing need to deal with those social conditions of poverty and injustice which often provide the breeding grounds for serious crime. We urge particularly the importance of restricting the easy availability of guns and other weapons of violence. We oppose the glamorizing of violence in entertainment, and we deplore the effect of this on children. We affirm the need for education to promote respect for the human dignity of all people" (*Statement on Capital Punishment*, #21).

The abolition of the death penalty will not provide a quick fix to the problem of crime, but neither will a new series of executions. Sooner or later, our society must deal with the many conditions that accelerate crime and violence in the nation. Christians, followers of the One who forgave his executioners, have a special mission to show compassion for crime's victims and true forgiveness for those who injure us. The Church calls us to be realistic about crime and its effects but honest about the limits and value of punishment, especially punishment that takes human life.

Amid the often pessimistic accounts of violence in our society, the U.S. bishops have offered a balanced perspective about crime. "Society cannot tolerate an ethic that uses violence to make a point, settle grievances, or help us get what we want. But the path to a more peaceful future is found in a rediscovery of personal responsibility, respect for human life and human dignity, and a recommitment to social justice. The best antidote to violence is hope. People with a stake in society do not destroy communities" (*Confronting a Culture of Violence*, p. 21).

For Further Discussion

1. The U.S. bishops have said that they oppose the death penalty under the "present circumstances." Should capital punishment depend on society's times?

2. The U.S. bishops have urged the Church to "provide a community of faith and trust in which God's grace can heal the personal and spiritual wounds caused by crime." What could a parish do for the victims of crime?

3. Catholic teaching suggests many long-term solutions to the problems of crime and violence. What short-term measures might be taken to reduce violence?

CHAPTER 3

POVERTY: SCOURGE AND BLESSING

The United States is a land of peculiar economic contrasts: our nation has created the greatest wealth the world has ever known, yet the infant-mortality rates of some of our cities rank with those of underdeveloped nations. Despite the tremendous productivity of our economic system, more than thirty million people remain poor. Without discounting the achievements of our country, Christians are today being called to look at the human consequences of our economic decisions, especially those that affect the poor.

A few statistics help illustrate the story. More than one-third of all families headed by women are poor, according to figures quoted in the U.S. Catholic bishops' 1986 *Economic Justice for All: Pastoral Letter on Catholic Social Teaching and the U.S. Economy*. One out of every four children under six years old in our country lives below the poverty line. For black children under six, the poverty rate is one in two. The bottom one-fifth of U.S. society draws only 4.7 percent of the nation's income, while the top one-fifth earns 42.9 percent.

The bishops wrote their letter not to condemn the United States or its economic system, but to urge that Catholics and other citizens face the reality of poverty and marshal the resources of our country to build a better society. As the bishops clearly stated, while Catholic social teaching does not demand absolute economic equality, a great disparity of wealth among people undermines a sense of community and makes it more difficult to meet the needs of the poor. Furthermore, "no one may claim the name Christian and be comfortable in the face of the hunger, homelessness, insecurity, and injustice found in this country and the world" (*Economic Justice for All,* #27).

Poverty in Scripture

Poverty is such a concern to Christians because our Scripture and tradition teach us "that the justice of a society is tested by the treatment of the poor," as the bishops explained in their brief pastoral message that accompanies *Economic Justice for All.* The Scriptures, especially the Old Testament prophets, are filled with exhortations to care for the poor. As part of their covenant with Yahweh, the Hebrew people were responsible for treating one another justly and for caring for the needs of the poorest among them: the widows and orphans. "Throughout the Bible, material poverty is a misfortune and a cause of sadness. A constant biblical refrain is that the poor must be cared for and protected and that when they are exploited, God hears their cries (Prv 22:22–23)" (*Economic Justice for All,* #49).

In his life and ministry, Jesus continued the prophetic tradition by reminding the Jewish people of their obligations to others and to God. Quoting Isaiah, Jesus defined his mission from the beginning as bringing "'good news to the poor'" (Luke 4:18). Jesus told the crowd on the hillside, "Blessed are you who are poor, for yours is the kingdom of God" (Luke 6:20)—a passage that is often misunderstood to be an approval of poverty. "When Jesus calls the poor 'blessed,'" explained the U.S. bishops, "he is not praising their condition of poverty, but their openness to God" (*Economic Justice for All*, #50).

Jesus not only spoke good news to the poor, he also warned his disciples of the dangers of riches. The parable of the wealthy farmer (Luke 12:16–21) shows how abundance can breed arrogance and a disregard for the needs of others. Pope John Paul II has used the parable of the Rich Man and Lazarus (Luke 16:19–31) to portray the relationship of the underdeveloped world to the developed nations. In the parable of the Last Judgment (Matthew 25:31–46), Jesus made it plain that our treatment of the "least" of society is in reality our treatment of him.

In their pastoral letter *Economic Justice for All,* the U.S. bishops echoed these warnings about wealth for our society: "The great wealth of the United States can easily blind us to the poverty that exists in this nation and the destitution of hundreds of millions of people in other parts of the world. Americans are challenged today as never before to develop the inner freedom to resist the temptation constantly to seek more" (#75). Church teaching does not demand that we give up all possessions but that we balance our needs with the needs of others. The bishops want us to think about how well our society is doing and how we might do better.

Poverty and the Catholic Tradition

The U.S. bishops have drawn upon a tradition of concern for the poor that dates from the exhortations on almsgiving by the early Christians and continues through the philosophical writings of the Middle Ages to the first of the modern social-teaching documents, *On the Condition of Workers* (1891) by Pope Leo XIII. According to that tradition, we all have social obligations to care for our needy sisters and brothers as well as to contribute to the common good through our productive capabilities. Corresponding to those duties are certain individual human rights that society must protect. Pope John XXIII outlined these rights in his encyclical *Peace on Earth* (1963).

Echoing Pope John, the U.S. bishops in *Economic Justice for All* cited as fundamental the rights to free speech, assembly, and movement from place to place—all basic civil and political rights guaranteed by the Constitution of the United States. But the pope and the bishops also named certain social and economic rights as necessary for a minimum level of dignity in society, including the rights to life, food, shelter, clothing, medical care, and employment. While in the United States there is wide agreement on what constitutes basic civil and political rights, no such consensus exists for social and economic rights. Realizing that there can be legitimate differences of opinion about how best to promote human dignity and protect economic rights, the bishops nevertheless insisted that there can be no disagreement on basic moral objectives.

"The challenge of this pastoral letter," wrote the bishops, "is not merely to think differently but also to act differently" (accompanying pastoral message to *Economic Justice for All,* #25). In the realm of action, the Church has a long, worldwide tradition on which to build, having raised up edifying examples of women and men in every age who have given their lives in heroic service to the poor. The first hospitals were established to care for the indigent sick and dying. In the United States, the work of the St. Vincent de Paul Society and Catholic Charities is well known. The involvement of Christians in corporal works of mercy gives eloquent witness to the abiding belief that " 'just as you did it to one of the least of these who are members of my family, you did it to me' " (Matthew 25:40).

The "Preferential Option for the Poor"

Charitable service to the poor will always be a necessary and important work for Christian churches. However, the Church today is asking that we take another step, for "charity requires more than alleviating misery. It demands genuine love for the person in need. It should probe the meaning of suffering and provoke a response that seeks to remedy causes" (*Economic Justice for All*, #356).

Following other Church leaders, the U.S. bishops used the term "preferential option for the poor" and were careful to explain that this is neither a condemnation of the affluent nor a choice to side with the poor against another social class. Instead, "the prime purpose of this special commitment to the poor is to enable them to become active participants in the life of society. It is to enable *all* persons to share in and contribute to the common good. The 'option for the poor,' therefore, is not an adversarial slogan that pits one group or class against another. Rather it states that the deprivation and powerlessness of the poor wounds the whole community" (*Economic Justice for All*, #88).

Similarly, Pope John Paul II addressed our response to the poor in *On the Hundredth Anniversary of* Rerum Novarum, his encyclical commemorating the anniversary of Pope Leo XIII's *On the Condition of Workers* (1891). "Love for others, and in the first place love for the poor, in whom the Church sees Christ himself, is made concrete in the *promotion of justice*," wrote the pope. "Justice will never be fully attained unless people see in the poor person, who is asking for help in order to survive, not an annoyance or a burden, but an opportunity for showing kindness and a chance for greater enrichment" (*On the Hundredth Anniversary,* #58). This perspective sees the poor as an essential part of the whole community.

Accordingly, our efforts to assist the poor must go beyond simple charitable giving. "It is not merely a matter of 'giving from one's surplus,' but of helping entire peoples which are presently excluded or marginalized to enter into the sphere of economic and human development," insisted Pope John Paul II. "For this to happen, it is not enough to draw on the surplus goods which in fact our world abundantly produces; it requires above all a change of lifestyles, of models of production and consumption, and of the established structures of power which today govern society" (*On the Hundredth Anniversary,* #58).

Poverty and Participation

One of the most important contributions of *Economic Justice for All* is that it calls not only for new measures to deal with poverty, but for a new way of looking at poverty and the poor. Poverty is not just a lack of goods; therefore, it cannot be "solved" just by rearranging wealth. To realize their full potential, people need to participate in and contribute to society. The poor must participate even in those programs that are designed to help them rise out of poverty. The bishops have urged us to "seek solutions that enable the poor to help themselves through such means as employment. Paternalistic programs which do too much *for* and too little *with* the poor are to be avoided" (#188).

The U.S. bishops have much experience with self-help programs, for since 1970 they have sponsored the Campaign for

Human Development (CHD), the nation's largest and most successful funding program for self-help groups of low-income people. More than $120 million, raised in annual collections in U.S. parishes, have been given to such groups across the nation.

The CHD program is based on the understanding that poverty is not just a lack of material resources. Bringing low-income people together so that they can help themselves, CHD is successful because it empowers the poor by restoring their hope and self-confidence.

Participation for all is a key concept of the bishops' vision. Without the sense of power and self-worth that comes from contributing to society, people will turn to violence and self-destructive behaviors like alcohol and drug abuse. It is relatively easy to give people the necessities of physical existence; it is harder, but no less important, to offer them a chance to contribute.

Seeking Solutions on Many Levels

Catholic social teaching sees many dimensions to the problems generated by poverty and their possible solutions. On the personal level, the poor can seek employment or education and training to better their lives, while the non-poor can offer direct service in the form of corporal works of mercy. On the group level, low-income people can join together in self-help or community groups like those funded by CHD. Likewise, churches and other organizations can pool their talents and resources to support such self-help efforts. Finally, the Church believes that government has a role to play in addressing social problems.

This layered approach to social responsibility reflects a principle of Catholic social teaching known as "subsidiarity," from the Latin noun meaning "help." Subsidiarity means that government has a right and even a duty to intervene in social affairs, but only in a limited way, when absolutely necessary to "help" meet genuine social needs.

"The Church opposes all statist and totalitarian approaches to socioeconomic questions," the bishops stated. "Social life is richer than governmental power can encompass" (*Economic Justice for All,* #121). Reflecting the U.S. bishops' confidence in the principle of subsidiarity, *Economic Justice for All* outlines the responsibilities of individuals and of key economic groups such as labor unions and managers. But the document also notes an important role for the government. "Society as a whole and in all its diversity is responsible for building up the common good," wrote the bishops. "But it is government's role to guarantee the minimum conditions that make this rich social activity possible, namely, human rights and justice" (#122).

The U.S. bishops named four priorities for our society's response to the poor:

1. The fulfillment of the basic needs of the poor
2. An increase in active social participation by the poor and marginalized members of society
3. A greater investment of wealth and talent in ways that can directly benefit the poor
4. The evaluation of governmental policies in light of their effect on the poor

To explain when and how government might intervene in social affairs, the bishops elaborated on the idea of subsidiarity: "This principle states that, in order to protect basic justice, government should undertake only those initiatives which exceed the capacity of individuals or private groups acting independently. Government should not replace or destroy smaller communities and individual initiative. Rather it should help them to contribute more effectively to social well-being and supplement their activity when the demands of justice exceed their capacities" (*Economic Justice for All*, #124).

Poverty and Policy

The U.S. Catholic Conference (USCC), the public-policy organization of the U.S. bishops, has often taken policy stands on specific legislative issues. The USCC, for example, participated in efforts to raise the minimum wage and to extend Aid to Families with Dependent Children. Such decisions represent specific assessments of social policy in light of the principles of Catholic teaching.

The bishops' public-policy stands offer examples of how the principles of Catholic teaching might be enfleshed in laws and institutions. They are not suggesting a political ideology for the Church or a set of specific rules for government involvement in economic life. Rather, they insist that public-policy directions "will depend on an assessment of specific needs and the most effective ways to address them" (*Economic Justice for All*, #124). This pragmatism is not just a public-relations ploy; it is a result of a Christian view of social progress.

"No utopia is possible on this earth; but as believers in the redemptive love of God and as those who have experienced God's forgiving mercy," wrote the bishops, "we know that God's providence is not and will not be lacking to us today" (#364). The kingdom of love to which we are called in faith is not a reign of earthly perfection but of compassion. In other words, Christians cannot base their efforts for the poor on some secular criterion of success. It seems safe to say that poverty and economic injustice will not be wiped out in our lifetimes. Perhaps that is what Jesus meant when he said "'you always have the poor with you'" (Matthew 26:11). Our efforts are unlikely to produce sudden or sweeping changes, but if we let ourselves be motivated by love, progress can occur, and a more human society can emerge.

Love of Poverty, Love for the Poor

Jesus' life and ministry were the clearest expression of love for the poor. "The example of Jesus poses a number of challenges to the contemporary Church," wrote the bishops. "It imposes a prophetic mandate to speak for those who have no one to speak for them, to be a defender of the defenseless, who in biblical terms are the poor. It also demands a compassionate vision that enables the Church to see things from the side of the poor and powerless, and to assess lifestyle, policies and social institutions in terms of their impact on the poor. It summons the Church also to be an instrument in assisting people to experience the liberating power of God in their own lives, so that they may respond to the Gospel in freedom and dignity. Finally, and most radically, it calls for an emptying of self, both individually and corporately, that allows the Church to experience the power of God in the midst of poverty and powerlessness" (*Economic Justice for All*, #52).

This last challenge to the Church represents a significant practical and theological shift for U.S. Catholics. After generations of Catholic immigrants have successfully struggled to overcome poverty in their own families, a new predominantly middle-class church is now being told that we need to empty ourselves to experience God in our lives. The bishops said little more about what this might mean, but it is clear that the "option for the poor" is intended to heighten our awareness of God in our midst. If we turn to the poor to serve them and make their concerns our own, the bishops seem to be saying, we will encounter the face of Christ.

The U.S. Catholic Worker Movement, founded by Dorothy Day and Peter Maurin, is based on what has been called the "gentle personalism" of service to the poor. Catholic Worker houses of hospitality strive to treat the homeless poor with dignity and respect. On a one-to-one basis, Catholic Worker staff try to heal the wounds of poverty by caring for the poor as contemporary incarnations of Christ. At the same time, the Catholic Worker Movement has criticized the economic system that has abandoned these poorest of the poor.

Encountering the Reality of Poverty

Poverty and the poor should not be romanticized. The poor sometimes receive compassion with gratitude, sometimes with resentment. Sometimes they display a tremendous faith, sometimes despair and resignation. They sometimes seem to have a lot of strength, sometimes little. But for citizens of the United States, the poor have a great lesson to teach: namely, that wealth is not absolute security, nor is poverty a hopeless condition. Service to the poor can be a great eyeopener: either the poor will minister to us, or to minister to them, we will discover our need for God.

Are the U.S. bishops asking too much of us when they say we need to be involved in overcoming poverty in our country? Pope John Paul II has gone even further: "Every individual is called upon to play his or her part" in "a campaign to be conducted by peaceful means, in order to secure development in peace, in order to safeguard nature itself and the world around us" (*On Social Concern*, #47). None of us is expected to save the world, only to do "our part." Catholic teaching reminds us that we have talents and we build careers not simply to enhance our own standard of living, but to give something back to the human community that has nurtured us and given us the opportunity to advance.

Poverty is not simply something to be eliminated, nor are we to keep the poor at a safe distance. We all have something to learn from contact with the poor and from looking at the world through their eyes. For one thing, each of us is perhaps a little more like the poor than we would like to admit. All of us experience some measure of powerlessness, insufficiency, and dependence. At the very least, we are all dependent on God. Though it is right and necessary that each of us do all we can to care for ourselves and those entrusted to us, no one is so self-reliant or powerful that he or she can manage without the help of others. A personal encounter with the poor is a good way to be reminded of that.

For Further Discussion

1. If human beings have economic rights, should the government be responsible for meeting the basic needs of the poor?

2. Experience something of the reality of poverty by working in a food pantry or a shelter for the homeless or just by visiting a bus depot in any major city. How do experiences like these bring you closer to God?

3. Homeowners receive a tax break if they are paying off a mortgage. Is that fair when the needs of the poor are not being met?

4. Over the past three decades, the U.S. economy has lost tens of thousands of low-skilled jobs that paid well enough to support a family, the very kinds of jobs the poor need. Should the government encourage industries that can provide such jobs, supplement family income through cash payments, or provide a safety net when such employment disappears?

CHAPTER 4

WAR, PEACE, AND CHRISTIAN CONSCIENCE

———

Our national awareness of the threat of war waxes and wanes depending on a whole range of worldwide events and local conditions. No sooner did the threat from the Soviet Union evaporate in the late 1980s than we became embroiled in a war in the Persian Gulf. Because the United States has economic or political interests in or near the world's major trouble spots, war and the threat of war is never very far away.

A very different international order faced the United States when the U.S. Catholic bishops first decided to write *The Challenge of Peace: God's Promise and Our Response*. The United States was poised at an ominous crossroads: in a spectacle observed the world over, Iran seized U.S. hostages, and Americans boiled with frustration; and the Soviet Army had invaded Afghanistan, causing relations between the two superpowers to deteriorate. Ronald Reagan consequently ran a successful campaign for the presidency, pledging to boost military spending and restore U.S. prestige around the world.

As government leaders openly discussed the possibility of "winning" a nuclear war, nerves that had grown used to the awesome presence of nuclear weaponry suddenly frayed. In those European nations regarded as the likely nuclear battlegrounds, grassroots movements against nuclear missiles brought hundreds of thousands of people into the streets. A native of Poland, Pope John Paul II repeatedly spoke out against warfare as a solution to human problems and reiterated the Vatican's opposition to the use of nuclear weapons.

A Pastoral Letter Draws Attention

While many people were speaking out against the dangers of war, and nuclear weaponry in particular, others regarded the issue essentially as a political and military problem—certainly not a matter on which Church leaders had anything to offer. Although the U.S. bishops had for decades issued pastoral statements outlining Church teaching on various social matters, it is fair to say that *The Challenge of Peace* received more national attention than all the rest of the bishops' social commentaries put together.

The Challenge of Peace is not only a forthright statement of Church teaching that came at a moment of intense national and international ferment on the arms race, it is a document intentionally shaped by public dialogue. The bishops could have simply written their statement behind closed doors, made it public, and awaited the response. Instead, they chose to engage in an open discussion of every conceivable aspect of this issue before fixing their statement in its final form.

Through three separate drafts, this document became more and more clarified, detailed, and, ultimately, effective. When it received final approval from the bishops in May 1983, two and one-half years after the process had begun, *The Challenge of Peace* not only had become a major statement of Catholic social teaching on war and peace, it also launched a new era of open dialogue between the U.S. Catholic Church and public policymakers in our country.

Two Modes of Self-Defense

Over the centuries, two responses to war have developed within the Church: pacifism and just war. Persecuted by the Roman military, the early Christians rejected warfare as incompatible with the gospel. After the persecutions ended, the Church gradually became an important part of Roman society. Augustine, noted fifth-century bishop and philosopher, argued persuasively that as a last resort in self-defense, and then only under strict limitations designed to reduce bloodshed, Christians could legitimately go to war.

Pacifism has held that Jesus' command to "turn the other cheek," combined with the fifth commandment, absolutely prohibits the taking of life, even in self-defense. Thus, people who believe in this response to war have chosen noncombat roles during wartime and nonviolent ways to resist aggression. "The vision of Christian nonviolence is not passive about injustice and the defense of the rights of others," the bishops insisted, "it rather affirms and exemplifies what it means to resist injustice through nonviolent methods" (*Challenge of Peace,* #116). In supporting the nonviolent option, the bishops urge greater study of nonviolent defensive strategies.

These two moral responses to war are "complementary" in that they both seek the common good—peace—while using different means. "The Christian has no choice but to defend peace, properly understood, against aggression," the bishops declared. "This is an inalienable obligation. It is the *how* of defending peace which offers moral options" (*Challenge of Peace,* #73). The bishops went on to insist that "no government, and certainly no Christian, may simply assume that" those who choose nonviolent defense "are mere pawns of conspiratorial forces or guilty of cowardice" (#73).

Although pacifism is an option for a private citizen, Church teaching holds that the obligations of governments are different from those of individual persons. "The Council and the popes have stated clearly," wrote the bishops, "that governments threatened by armed, unjust aggression must defend their people. This includes defense by armed force, if necessary, as a last resort" (*Challenge of Peace,* #75). Similarly, Church teaching has supported the use of armed force "as a last resort to put an end to an obvious and prolonged tyranny which is gravely damaging the fundamental rights of individuals and the common good" ("Instruction on Christian Liberation and Freedom," #79).

"Just-War" Theory

In developing the just-war theory, Augustine made a strong presumption against war as a solution to conflict and strictly limited the reasons why a nation could go to war. After exhausting all other means, the legitimate authority in a nation could declare war in defense against an unjust aggressor. Because war brings so much harm, Augustine said, it must be clear that a greater good will come as a result of the conflict.

Augustine also outlined two key moral principles governing the conduct of the war itself, principles that the U.S. bishops used in their analysis of nuclear war. These are the principles of discrimination—that the weapons of war be directed against unjust aggressors, not noncombatants—and of proportionality—that the harm caused by using a particular weapon or strategy in self-defense not exceed the good to be gained by its use.

The U.S. bishops applied the just-war theory to the modern military strategies made possible by nuclear weapons. After much discussion with military and political experts as well as moral theologians, the U.S. bishops concluded that "the first imperative is to prevent any use of nuclear weapons" (*Challenge of Peace*, #161). Any use of nuclear weapons, said the experts, no matter how carefully planned or delivered, would likely quickly evolve into a total thermonuclear destruction of most of the world. Such a consequence would certainly violate the principles of discrimination and proportionality.

Nor are nuclear exchanges the only type of combat capable of causing inordinate destruction. "The history of recent wars (even so-called 'minor' or 'limited' wars) has shown that conventional war can also become indiscriminate in conduct and disproportionate to any valid purpose," cautioned the bishops. "We do not want in any way to give encouragement to a notion of 'making the world safe for conventional war,' which introduces its own horrors" (*Challenge of Peace*, #217).

Reflecting ten years later on *The Challenge of Peace*, the U.S. bishops warned that the just-war theory could be misapplied. "The just-war tradition is not a weapon to be used to justify a political conclusion or a set of mechanical criteria that automatically yields a simple answer, but a way of moral reasoning to discern the ethical limits of action," they cautioned in their 1993 letter, *The Harvest of Justice Is Sown in Peace*. "Policy-makers, advocates and opponents need to be careful not to apply the tradition selectively, simply to justify their own positions."

The Debate over Deterrence

The bishops recognized that "the moral challenge posed by nuclear weapons is not exhausted by an analysis of their possible uses. Much of the political and moral debate of the nuclear age has concerned the strategy of deterrence" (*Challenge of Peace*, #162). Church teaching has evaluated and will continue to appraise deterrence strategy, or the maintenance of nuclear weapons systems as a means of preventing other countries from using their nuclear arsenals.

The dilemma of deterrence strategy is that it seems to have succeeded since 1945 in preventing the use of nuclear weapons. For the strategy to be credible, some conceivable use of nuclear weapons must be allowed. Yet, as the bishops themselves became convinced, any use of nuclear weapons is likely to be disastrous.

The Second Vatican Council expressed discomfort with the burgeoning arms race because of the tremendous economic resources being poured into nuclear weapons, which then spread across the world. Yet the council did not reject deterrence strategy or the possession of nuclear weapons. Speaking in 1979 for the bishops' conference in support of the SALT II arms-control agreement, Cardinal John Krol of Philadelphia asked that governments become dedicated to "continuing reductions in nuclear stockpiles and eventually to the phasing out altogether of nuclear deterrence and the threat of mutual-assured destruction" (*SALT II: A Statement of Support*, p. 197).

Pope John Paul II similarly expressed discomfort with deterrence in a message at the United Nations Second Special Session on Disarmament in June 1982. "In current conditions 'deterrence' based on balance, certainly not as an end in itself but as a step on the way toward a progressive disarmament, may still be judged morally acceptable. Nonetheless, in order to ensure peace," the pope emphasized, "it is indispensable not to be satisfied with this minimum which is always susceptible to the real danger of explosion" (quoted in *Challenge of Peace*, #173).

The bishops further clarified their position in "A Report on 'The Challenge of Peace' and Policy Developments 1983–1988," a report of the Ad Hoc Committee on the Moral Evaluation of Deterrence. Approved in June 1988, this report stated, "*The Challenge of Peace* has neither advocated any form of use nor has it condemned every conceivable use of nuclear weapons *a priori*. There is in the letter a narrow margin where use has been considered, not condemned, but hardly commended. From this narrow margin the pastoral moves to an evaluation of deterrence" (*A Report on "The Challenge of Peace,"* #40).

The U.S. Catholic bishops decided in *The Challenge of Peace* to give a "strictly conditioned moral acceptance" of deterrence strategy provided that it

1. had as its purpose the prevention of using nuclear weapons;
2. aimed not at superiority over potential adversaries but only sufficient strength to deter;
3. was a step toward progressive disarmament.

The bishops pledged themselves and called upon others to carefully evaluate each new proposed weapons system according to these criteria.

Building Peace

"We cannot consider [deterrence] adequate as a long-term basis for peace," the U.S. bishops wrote in *The Challenge of Peace* (#186). In reviewing the morality of deterrence five years later, the bishops made it clear that their conditional acceptance of deterrence "is not an endorsement of the status quo that we find inadequate and dangerous. It is a position that requires us to work for genuine and far-reaching changes in the policies that guide nuclear arsenals of the world" (*A Report on "The Challenge of Peace,"* p. 146).

In 1983, as an alternative to learning to live with nuclear deterrence, the bishops urged the United States to initiate nuclear-arms-reduction talks with the Soviet Union. History has shown that both the United States and the Soviet Union ultimately did decrease their nuclear stockpiles. Whether these first important steps will lead to progressive disarmament throughout the world remains to be seen, but it seems clear that *The Challenge of Peace* helped move public opinion and perhaps governmental policy to a greater acceptance of the need to slow the arms race.

Although *The Challenge of Peace* devotes a great deal of space to weapons and the circumstances of war, it has a great deal to say about the building of peace too. "Peace is not just the absence of war," said Pope John Paul II. "It involves mutual respect and confidence between peoples and nations. It involves collaboration and binding agreements. Like a cathedral, peace must be constructed patiently and with unshakable faith" (homily at Coventry, England, quoted in *Challenge of Peace,* #200).

Borrowing from the famous encyclical *Peace on Earth* of Pope John XXIII, the U.S. bishops explained that peace is the fruit of justice, whether within a particular society or in relations between nations. "The fundamental premise of world order in Catholic teaching," wrote the bishops, "is a theological truth: the unity of the human family—rooted in common creation, destined for the kingdom, and united by bonds of rights and duties" (*Challenge of Peace,* #236).

According to Pope John XXIII, nation-states are valuable insofar as they exercise legitimate political authority and thereby help build and preserve order. But even their value cannot obscure the fundamental unity of the human family. This unity is increasingly evident in the growing "interdependence" of nations for their basic needs. Self-sufficiency is no longer possible or desirable in our highly specialized, technologically advanced world. Church teaching regards the increasing interdependence of nations as a key feature of the contemporary world.

Interdependence is evident not only in the material goods nations can receive from other nations, but also in the degree to which war or drastic change abroad can disrupt domestic life. The instability of the nation-state system poses a concern to the bishops: "An important element missing from world order today is a properly constituted political authority with the capacity to shape our material interdependence in the direction of moral interdependence" (*Challenge of Peace*, #241). International institutions have yet to effectively reflect interdependence, a fact of economic life. This issue will be more thoroughly explored in chapter 8.

With the fall of the Soviet Union and the Warsaw Pact, the "United States should play a constructive role in making the United Nations and other international institutions more effective, responsible and responsive," said the U.S. bishops *(Harvest of Justice)*. "Effective multilateral institutions can relieve the United States of the burden, or the temptation, of becoming by itself the world's police force."

The Church and Peace

Despite the attention given to *The Challenge of Peace*, commentators have often overlooked the theological perspective from which the bishops addressed the problem of war and peace.

As they reminded us in their tenth-anniversary letter, "We should never forget that peace is not merely something that we ourselves as creatures do and can accomplish, but it is, in the ultimate analysis, a gift and a grace from God. By its nature, the gift of peace is not restricted to moments of prayer. It seeks to penetrate the corners of everyday life and to transform the world" *(Harvest of Justice)*.

To better prepare Catholics for their responsibilities as disciples of Christ in one of the world's nuclear powers, the bishops recommended special programs to educate people about the Church's teachings on war and peace. They also urged "all who would work to end the scourge of war to begin by defending life at its most defenseless, the life of the unborn" (*Challenge of Peace*, #289). Although they distinguished between killing to thwart an unjust aggressor and ending human life in the womb, the bishops warned against strategies of expedience that would result in millions of deaths.

Prayer and penance will convert our hearts and minds to work more energetically for peace. The U.S. bishops promoted a return to the traditional practice of prayer, penance, and almsgiving each Friday out of an urgent sense of the danger posed by nuclear weapons. "As a tangible sign of our need and desire to do penance we, for the cause of peace, commit ourselves to fast and abstinence on each Friday of the year" (*Challenge of Peace*, #298). They wrote, "The present nuclear arms race has distracted us from the words of the prophets, has turned us from peacemaking, and has focused our attention on a nuclear buildup leading to annihilation. We are called to turn back from this evil of total destruction and turn instead in prayer and penance toward God, toward our neighbor, and toward the building of a peaceful world" (#300).

One of the ways U.S. Catholics can manifest this turning

from nuclear destruction is to look at our past in a new way. "After the passage of nearly four decades and a concomitant growth in our understanding of the ever-growing horror of nuclear war, we must shape the climate of opinion which will make it possible for our country to express profound sorrow over the atomic bombing in 1945. Without that sorrow, there is no possibility of finding a way to repudiate future use of nuclear weapons or of conventional weapons in such military actions as would not fulfill just-war criteria" (*Challenge of Peace*, #302).

Conclusion

Questions of war and peace remain among the most serious issues facing U.S. citizens and Church members. "The best of America's values and actions continue to inspire other peoples' struggles for justice and freedom and contribute to building a more just world," said the U.S. bishops *(Harvest of Justice)*. "What the United States can offer the world and what the world desperately needs is creative engagement, a willingness to collaborate and a commitment to values that can build up the global community."

As we continue to ask whether or not our national policies are morally acceptable, even in the interests of national security, we will need the support our faith tradition can give us. "We are called to be peacemakers, not by some movement of the moment, but by our Lord Jesus," the bishops reminded us. "The content and context of our peacemaking is set, not by some political agenda or ideological program, but by the teaching of his Church" (*Challenge of Peace*, #333).

So often it is fear that keeps us from the task of becoming genuine peacemakers. Fear can quicken the desire to use violence to resolve a dispute, or it can make one willing to accept injustice to avoid suffering. As U.S. Catholics, we are especially challenged to make our national motto, "In God We Trust," the basis of fearless and true peacemaking in the coming years.

For Further Discussion

1. Facing the reality of nuclear weapons is essential if we are to control and not be controlled by them. Learn about one nuclear weapon system, such as the Trident submarine, and ask about its firepower, its likely targets, whether it is primarily defensive or offensive, and its advantages and dangers.

2. Attend a prayer service commemorating the nuclear bombings of Hiroshima and Nagasaki. If there is none in your area, organize a brief service that describes what happened and why, and then pray for healing, both for the Japanese victims and the U.S. decision makers.

3. Discuss whether or not U.S. military assistance to foreign countries ought to depend on "just-war" criteria. In other words, should our country be morally accountable for what is done with the weapons we provide?

4. One strategy about the use of military force concludes that to bring conflict to a swift conclusion, "overwhelming force" must be brought to bear on the enemy's ability to wage war. That ability, it is argued, depends not only on military resources (soldiers, weapons, and so on), but on the entire resources of the country (supplies of food and water, communications, psychological determination, and so forth). In such a strategy, can "civilian" targets be separated from "military" targets? Can this strategy be reconciled with the just-war theory?

CHAPTER 5

EQUALITY: ONE CREATOR, ONE DESTINY

———

The basic idea behind this chapter is simple and familiar: all people, regardless of any distinction—race, creed, sex, national origin, sexual preference, habit of thought, political party, and so on—must be treated with equal dignity because they have been created by God, redeemed by Christ, and called to spend eternity with God in heaven. Most of us agree, yet it is common to feel some measure of prejudice toward one group or another.

Philosophers tell us that it is difficult to recognize our common humanity because it contradicts the rich variety we experience in human society every day. Each of us is unique, yet we are a great deal like others. Unity and distinction exist side by side, and that can be hard to understand at times. Even within families, no matter how close they are, individuals can become painfully aware of just how different and sometimes isolated they are from one another.

Overcoming prejudice is not simply a matter of balancing philosophical concepts or improving one's understanding. According to many psychologists, prejudice is rooted in the human tendency to concentrate, however unintentionally, our own worst fears and insecurities in another person or group of people. The likely targets of this kind of psychological "projection" are those with whom we have something in common yet who are also distinct. Thus, Jews in Europe and African Americans in the United States have historically been targets of state-sanctioned discrimination and periodic violence.

Nor has the Church itself been immune from prejudice. For example, parishes and Catholic schools were segregated by race in many parts of our country prior to the passage of civil-rights legislation. Recent Vatican statements have taken important steps toward healing relations with our Jewish sisters and brothers whose mistreatment at the hands of Christians over the years is well documented. The past has many sobering reminders of how easily the sparks of prejudice can flame into horrible crimes.

Better understanding its call to be the living Body of Christ on earth and a light to the world, the Church has increasingly added its voice to those insisting upon equality. Important statements by the U.S. Catholic bishops and the Vatican have addressed racial prejudice and suggested ways to overcome it, and the Church continues to grapple with the problem of sexism and the ways in which it hinders women from assuming full equality and dignity in both the Church and society at large.

Racism in the United States

Faced with courage and honesty, the past can present a moving testimony of hope, for it is clear that we have come a long way. For example, celebrations of the fifth centenary of the coming of Europeans to North America provided an opportunity for U.S. Catholics to reflect on the past as well as look toward the future. The U.S. bishops in their statement *Heritage and Hope: Evangelization in the United States* acknowledged that the Church had made mistakes in its treatment of Native Americans, particularly in the lack of respect shown to native religions and traditions. At the same time, the bishops noted the good done by Christian missionaries and the strength with which Christianity has taken root among native peoples.

The purpose of looking at the past is not just to lament previous errors but to understand better how we arrived at the present and what we need to do to go forward. All of us in the United States need to appreciate how race relations have improved since World War II lest these gains be taken for granted. To be sure, there is a long way to go, but recalling how far we've come can give us the energy to continue to build true community in our land.

African slaves brought to and held in this country during the three hundred years of slavery were treated not as humans but as property. Because the treatment of slaves was virtually unrestricted, terrible indignities and punishments formed the normal routine of the slave economy. Not only did individuals suffer heartrending cruelties, the fabric of African-American society was damaged in ways that continue to cry out for healing.

After the Civil War, segregation almost immediately became law in many parts of the country. So-called "Jim Crow" laws ensured that white people would continue to enjoy a privileged status. Although racial violence was technically illegal, occasional lynchings, routine beatings, and threats restricted the activities and opportunities of former slaves and their children.

Racism also played a part in our relations with Native Americans, Mexicans, and the immigrants who have come to the United States during the last century.

The civil-rights movement in the 1960s brought about legislation that made it illegal to deny basic human rights to a racial group. Racial discrimination no longer has the respectability of being part of our legal system. Having removed prejudice from our law books, we now face the more difficult challenge of addressing the prejudice in our hearts.

Racism and the U.S. Church

Although many Catholics had leading roles in the struggle for racial equality in our country, the Catholic hierarchy for the most part was not involved in the civil-rights movement until the mid-1960s. A 1958 statement by the administrative board of the National Catholic Welfare Conference, as the bishops' conference was then called, did speak out against discrimination and segregation, but it warned against "rash impetuosity that would sacrifice the achievements of decades in ill-timed and ill-considered ventures" (*Discrimination and Christian Conscience,* #22). Preferring to work behind the scenes, the bishops urged Catholics to act "quietly, courageously, and prayerfully before it is too late" (#23).

Meeting a decade later in the wake of rioting touched off by the assassination of Dr. Martin Luther King, Jr., the bishops issued *Statement on National Race Crisis*. This pastoral letter has a tone of great urgency and calls on Catholics to cooperate with social and government organizations to provide education, jobs, housing, and welfare assistance for impoverished members of minority groups.

During the 1970s the crisis in race relations gave way to a period of relative quiet in which many black people and members of other ethnic minorities pursued newly opened opportunities for educational and career advancement. For the poor, however, the situation did not improve. The poverty rooted in the racist practices of the past persisted, even though rioting ceased to draw attention to it. In a major 1979 statement entitled *Brothers and Sisters to Us,* the U.S. Catholic bishops addressed the problem of racism, detailing how it affects the poor and what can be done about it.

The purpose of *Brothers and Sisters to Us* is evident in its opening line: "Racism is an evil which endures in our society and in our Church" (#1). Although recognizing many forms of discrimination in our society, the bishops addressed racism in particular and condemned it unequivocally. "Racism is not merely one sin among many," they wrote, "it is a radical evil that divides the human family and denies the new creation of a redeemed world" (#39). They also stated, "Racism is a sin: a sin that...blots out the image of God among specific members of the human family, and violates the fundamental human dignity of those called to be children of the same Father" (#9).

The bishops, aware that the country was in the midst of an economic downturn, were alarmed to see the disproportionate number of minority people among the poor and wished "to call attention to the persistent presence of racism and in particular to the relationship between racial and economic justice" (*Brothers and Sisters to Us,* #5). "The minority poor are seen as the dross of a postindustrial society—without skills, without motivation, without incentive" (#22). The bishops feared that in the absence of riots or large-scale demonstrations, an atmosphere of indifference to the plight of minorities had overshadowed the country, and these poor would be regarded as expendable.

In the 1960s, it sometimes appeared that the passage of legislation and the right social programs could overcome racism.

But by the time the bishops wrote *Brothers and Sisters to Us,* they knew better what we were up against. "It is important to realize in the case of racism that we are dealing with a distortion at the very heart of human nature. The ultimate remedy against evils such as this will not come solely from human effort. What is needed is the recreation of the human being according to the image revealed in Jesus Christ" (#30).

Racism and Healing in the Church

The importance of *Brothers and Sisters to Us* was not only its recognition of the connection between racism and poverty, but its admission of racism within the Church itself. The document calls upon the Church at every level to examine its own conscience and to "proclaim to all that the sin of racism defiles the image of God and degrades the sacred dignity of humankind which has been revealed by the mystery of the Incarnation" (#36).

In response to that sin, the bishops urged action by individuals, by the Church, and by society as a whole. "As individuals we should try to influence the attitudes of others by expressly rejecting racial stereotypes, racial slurs, and racial jokes. We should influence the members of our families, especially our children, to be sensitive to authentic human values and cultural contributions of each racial grouping in our country" (*Brothers and Sisters to Us,* #42).

The bishops asked the Church to boost non-white leadership and vocations, foster a diversity of liturgical expression, adopt affirmative-action programs, and maintain Catholic schools serving minority communities. Since the approval of *Brothers and Sisters to Us,* there has in fact been an evident renewal in the Church's ministry to Native Americans through the Tekakwitha Conference, to Hispanics through the national *Encuentro* gatherings, and to African Americans, most recently through the National Black Catholic Congress. Efforts like these affirm the minority presence within the Church and acknowledge the gifts these various cultures bring to the Body of Christ.

From society, the bishops hope for a renewed commitment to such basic human needs as employment, adequate income, housing, education, and healthcare. These very concerns formed a significant dimension of the 1986 pastoral letter, *Economic Justice for All,* which addresses the relationship between Catholic social teaching and the U.S. economy.

The Vatican's Statement on Racism

If *Brothers and Sisters to Us* is an important reminder that racism is still a problem in the United States, a 1988 statement from the Vatican makes it clear that racism is still a problem in the world at large. At the request of Pope John Paul II, the Pontifical Justice and Peace Commission wrote *The Church and Racism: Towards a More Fraternal Society.* This document provides a well-written overview of the history of racism and makes suggestions for action in today's world.

The historical perspective of *The Church and Racism* is not a complete history of racism or of the Church's relation to it; rather, it shows the consistent position of Church teaching. Like *Brothers and Sisters to Us,* the Vatican document acknowledges that there is and has been racism among Christians, but that the gospel and Church doctrine unequivocally condemn it. "Faith in the one God, Creator and Redeemer of all humankind made in his image and likeness, constitutes the absolute and unescapable negation of any racist ideologies" (*Church and Racism,* #19).

Defining racism as an "awareness of the biologically determined superiority of one's own race or ethnic group" (#2), *The Church and Racism* cites some contemporary examples of racist behavior. South African apartheid, in which the law sanctions racial discrimination, is named as the worst form of contemporary racism. Echoing the words of Pope John Paul II, the document calls upon all parties to work together to bring justice and peace to that country.

The Vatican cited the U.S. civil-rights movement and the statements of the U.S. bishops as examples of social progress and responsible Church leadership. The importance of such social evolution is that without it, there can be no lasting peace. "History shows," reads *The Church and Racism,* "that the prolonged failure to recognize human rights almost always ends in outbreaks of uncontrollable violence" (#32).

The Vatican spoke about racism to help society progress. "While she [the Church] is not afraid to examine lucidly the evils of racism and disapprove of them, even to those who are responsible for them, she also seeks to understand how these people could have reached that point. She would like to help them find a reasonable way out" (*Church and Racism,* #27).

Equality of Male and Female

The U.S. Catholic bishops set out in 1983 to write a pastoral letter to address the concerns of women who experience a "second-class status" in the Church as well as in society. After several years of consultations with scholars, theologians, and women of varied backgrounds and perspectives, the bishops decided not to issue a pastoral letter, but instead to release a committee draft letter as a basis for further discussion and reflection. Having examined a wide spectrum of contemporary analysis and opinion, the committee "came to see the need for a deeper analysis of how sexual difference is related to equality between men and women in theory and in practice" (*One in Christ Jesus*, #6).

Why should a "deeper analysis" be necessary at this time? Changes in modern society have brought about a reconsideration of the role of women and, by extension, the role of men. Pope John XXIII in his 1963 encyclical *Peace on Earth* noted that the increased public role of women was a distinctive characteristic of the modern age. "Since women are becoming ever more conscious of their human dignity, they will not tolerate being treated as inanimate objects or mere instruments, but claim, both in domestic and public life, the rights and duties that befit a human person" (*Peace on Earth*, #41).

The Second Vatican Council in its *Pastoral Constitution on the Church in the Modern World* noted that "every type of discrimination, whether social or cultural, whether based on sex, race, color, social condition, language, or religion, is to be overcome and eradicated as contrary to God's intent....Such is the case of the woman who is denied the right and freedom to choose a husband, to embrace a state of life, or to acquire an education or cultural benefits equal to those recognized for men" (#29).

Responding to concerns expressed in the 1987 synod of bishops, Pope John Paul II wrote a "meditation" called *On the Dignity and Vocation of Women*. "One of [the bishops'] recommendations was for a further study of the anthropological and theological bases that are needed in order to solve the problems connected with the meaning and dignity of being a woman and being a man," wrote the pope. "It is a question of understanding the reason for and the consequences of the Creator's decision that the human being should always and only exist as a woman or a man" (*On the Dignity and Vocation of Women*, #1). This document explores Mary's role in Christian salvation and her meaning for the Church and for all humankind, particularly women. Although he is concerned that certain forms of feminism might lead women to become "masculinized" and lose their "essential richness," the pope repeatedly asserted the equal humanity of men and women. For example, he described marriage as "mutual self-giving" in which women and men help one another discover their true selves.

Pope John Paul II recognizes that such mutuality between men and women does not always exist and that women have suffered and continue to suffer much by the denial of their dignity and freedom. Men are challenged particularly not to regard women as objects of lust nor abandon them should they become pregnant (*On the Dignity and Vocation of Women*, #14).

Against Sexism

Although it was not adopted as the position of the entire U.S. bishops' conference, the third draft of the proposed pastoral letter on the concerns of women, *One in Christ Jesus*, was released as a committee report to stimulate further discussion. In brief, *One in Christ Jesus* defines sexism as "the erroneous conviction 'that one sex, male or female, is superior to the other in the very order of creation or by the very nature of things'" (#12). The report does not conclude that there is no difference between women and men, but that there is a fundamental equality of men and women as creative beings.

"It is our conviction that the equality of women and men as persons is best served not by disregarding sexual difference but by taking this gift and reality into account," wrote the committee. "What must be overcome is the disorder that enters relationships between the sexes on account of sin" (*One in Christ Jesus*, #16). As a result of the sin of sexism, women suffer in our society in a variety of ways: discrimination in employment, abusive treatment in the home, lack of appreciation for women's gifts, and so on. The more difficult questions have to do with the way in which society and the Church should take action to counter the effects of sexism.

The issue of women's ordination epitomizes these questions. Despite his belief in the equal dignity of men and women, Pope John Paul II holds that the Church is not free to change the tradition of an exclusively male priesthood. The explanations most often given for this tradition are that Jesus called men to be the first apostles and that it is crucial to such sacraments as the Eucharist that a man act "in the person of Christ." The Vatican has instructed the U.S. bishops to accept the position enunciated by the pope and to end all dialogue on the matter of women's ordination.

Those who regard women's ordination as a right based upon the equality of men and women are unlikely to accept the Church's official position, even though it is based on the traditional role of priest, not on any supposed superiority of men over women. In the words of the bishops' committee, "The priest's distinctive role in the Church's sacramental life, as representing Christ who continues to call us to be Church through his ministry of word and sacrament, does not remove him from baptismal equality in the community of the faithful" (*One in Christ Jesus*, #128).

The Future of Equality

Neither the pope's meditation nor the bishops' committee letter can resolve all contemporary women's issues or end sexism in the Church and society. Instead, they can contribute to the reappraisal of what it means to be a woman, a reappraisal that necessarily affects what it means to be a man. The Church will certainly continue to proclaim that God created male and female as distinct sexual beings equal in dignity and personhood. Further anthropological study of the interaction of human biology and culture will no doubt increase our understanding of the meaning of sexuality and gender identity. At the same time, it is imperative for the Church to receive and appreciate the gifts of women so that it can continue to proclaim the gospel to the world.

For Further Discussion

1. What groups are the objects of prejudice in your community? Talk it over with someone else, or pray about it with the intention of simply becoming aware of it.

2. Justice demands that we make some effort to atone for the evil we have done. Does society have the obligation to make up for past social injustices done to groups of people? If not, does that mean that some groups must continue to suffer the effects of past discrimination?

3. Does affirmative action effectively address the ill effects of past discrimination or is it unfair discrimination?

4. In what ways, if any, does your being male or female affect your life? How do the expectations of others influence your behavior?

CHAPTER 6

THE STEWARDSHIP OF CREATION

———

The list of potential environmental catastrophes is familiar: global warming could drastically change the earth's climate and food production; depletion of the ozone layer could erode a shield against harmful ultraviolet rays from the sun; toxic wastes could contaminate the food chain and drinking water; and so on. Never has the environment seemed more at risk than in this age of technological sophistication.

Indeed, science and technology have given humankind the tools to measure and assess the environmental impact of our actions. These can help us make better choices if we do not lose hope and become fatalistic. Our Christian tradition teaches us that we must cherish the gift of creation as we use it for the purpose our Creator intended.

Creation: God's Gift to Humanity

In the Judeo-Christian creation story, human beings, made in God's own image, are the pinnacle, indeed the purpose, of creation. Christian concern for the environment begins with understanding the world as God's gift to us.

After having created the man and the woman, "God blessed them, and God said to them: 'Be fruitful and multiply, and fill the earth and subdue it; and have dominion over the fish of the sea and over the birds of the air and over every living thing that moves upon the earth.' God said, 'See, I have given you every plant yielding seed that is upon the face of all the earth, and every tree with seed in its fruit; you shall have them for food. And to every beast of the earth, and to every bird in the air, and to everything that creeps on the earth, everything that has the breath of life, I have given every green plant for food.' And it was so. God saw everything that he had made, and indeed, it was very good" (Genesis 1:28–31).

Pope John Paul II, known to be an avid hiker and outdoorsman, has repeatedly urged world leaders to enact policies to protect the environment. In his 1987 encyclical *On Social Concern,* which addresses worldwide social and economic development, the pope made several important references to the environment. The following observations are part of his reflections:

1. animals, plants, and natural elements cannot be used "simply as one wishes, according to one's own economic needs. On the contrary, one must take into account *the nature of each being* and of its *mutual connection* in an ordered system, which is precisely the 'cosmos'";
2. natural resources are limited;

3. industrialization too often results in environmental pollution (*On Social Concern,* #34).

"The dominion granted to man [humankind] by the Creator," the pope went on to say, "is not an absolute power, nor can one speak of a freedom to 'use and misuse,' or to dispose of things as one pleases. The limitation imposed from the beginning by the Creator...and expressed symbolically by the prohibition not to 'eat of the fruit of the tree' (cf. Gen 2:16–17) shows clearly enough that, when it comes to the natural world, we are subject not only to biological laws but also to moral ones, which cannot be violated with impunity" (*On Social Concern,* #34).

Stewardship

Stewardship, a concept well known in the Protestant tradition and increasingly familiar to Catholics, can help us understand our responsibilities in an ordered universe. Stewardship refers to the responsible use of one's gifts. One of the most striking scriptural references to stewardship is found in a parable Jesus told his disciples as he traveled to Jerusalem for the last time (Luke 19:11–27). A rich noble was called away temporarily, so he gave an equal amount of money to each of ten servants and told them to invest it for him. Upon the master's return, those who had gained him a profit were praised and rewarded, but the servant who had buried the money for fear of making a bad investment was scorned and punished.

In his *On Social Concern,* Pope John Paul II urged us to reflect soberly on this parable. Those who have much—talent, riches, education, technology, and so forth—are not free to do nothing with their wealth. Instead, they must use it so that it can bear fruit. Stewardship, then, cannot mean simply avoiding waste; it implies that we use the gifts we have for the right purposes.

Considered as our most precious gift, creation itself is to be used for the good of all people, according to Catholic social teaching. In the *Pastoral Constitution on the Church in the Modern World,* the Second Vatican Council stated that "God intended the earth and all that it contains for the use of every human being and people....Whatever the forms of ownership may be, as adapted to the legitimate institutions of people according to diverse and changeable circumstances, attention must always be paid to the universal purpose for which created goods are meant. In using them, therefore, a man [person] should regard his [or her] lawful possessions not merely as his [or her] own but also as common property in the sense that they should accrue to the benefit of not only himself [or herself] but of others" (#69).

Private Property and Common Good

The Second Vatican Council reaffirmed the Church's traditional support of private property as an expression of human freedom. As it provides incentives for "carrying on one's function and duty," private property is also "a kind of prerequisite for civil liberties" (*Church in the Modern World,* #71). Private property is good not simply because it benefits the individual, but because it contributes to the good of society as a whole.

The common good must be part of the discussion of environmental stewardship because private decisions can have such immense social consequences. Those consequences, as Pope John Paul II reminded farmers during his 1979 visit to the United States, affect future generations: "You who live in the heartland of America have been entrusted with some of the earth's best land: the soil so rich in minerals, the climate so favorable for producing bountiful crops, with fresh water and unpolluted land all around you. You are stewards of some of the most important resources God has given to the world. Therefore conserve the land well, so that your children's children and generations after them will inherit an even richer land than was entrusted to you" (Quoted in *Strangers and Guests*, #62).

To encourage stewardship of the land during a period of great change in agricultural practice, the bishops of ten Midwestern states wrote *Toward Community in the Heartland: Strangers and Guests* in 1980. A fundamental concept of the pastoral letter as well as its title are drawn from a passage in the Book of Leviticus: "The land shall not be sold in perpetuity," Yahweh told the Israelites, "for the land is mine; with me you are but aliens and tenants [strangers and guests]" (Leviticus 25:23).

The land belongs to God, said the bishops, and "those who are God's stewards on the land are also **co-creators** with God in guiding the land's productive power and in conserving the land's natural gifts. As co-creators, God's stewards help the land fulfill the purpose for which God created it: to help satisfy the physical, social and spiritual needs of God's creatures" (*Strangers and Guests*, #55).

The bishops urged that the concept of stewardship be applied not only to the natural resources of agriculture but also to the agricultural community itself. Accordingly, they urged that land be equitably divided, that those who work it someday come to own it, and that land-use planning consider the social as well as environmental impacts.

Toward an Environmental Theology

As science and technology continue to make fundamental changes in the way we produce what we need for survival, the Church will also continue to insist that humankind care for the gift of creation. In their *Renewing the Earth: An Invitation to Reflection and Action on Environment in Light of Catholic*

Social Teaching, the U.S. Catholic bishops sought to stimulate a discussion of environmental concerns. Of particular concern for the bishops is the connection "between natural ecology and social ecology. The web of life is one....Our tradition calls us to protect the life and dignity of the human person, and it is increasingly clear that this task cannot be separated from the care and defense of all of creation" (*Renewing the Earth,* p. 5).

Acknowledging that Catholic social teaching does not offer a complete environmental ethic, the bishops believe the following principles drawn from that tradition "can serve as the basis for Catholic engagement and dialogue with science, the environmental movement, and other communities of faith and good will" (*Renewing the Earth,* p. 6):

1. All of creation is a gift from God. Endowed with intelligence and creativity, human beings are both part of nature and caretakers of it. "Stewardship implies that we must both care for creation according to standards that are not of our own making and at the same time be resourceful in finding ways to make the earth flourish" (*Renewing the Earth,* p. 6).

2. Respect for nature and respect for human life are linked. The natural world in all its variety is testimony to the goodness of the Creator and is worthy of respect. "Accordingly, it is appropriate that we treat other creatures and the natural world not just as means to human fulfillment but also as God's creatures, possessing an independent value, worthy of our respect and care" (*Renewing the Earth,* p. 7).

3. The environmental crisis makes it clear that the principle of the common good must extend to the entire globe. Governments must have a role, Pope John Paul II has

said, in providing "for the defense and preservation of the common good such as the natural and human environments, which cannot be safeguarded simply by market forces" (*On the Hundredth Anniversary,* #40).

4. Solidarity, called by Pope John Paul II "*a firm and persevering determination* to commit oneself to the *common good*" (*On Social Concern,* #38), requires us to sacrifice some of our own self-interest for the good of others. This is particularly so in relations between developed and developing nations.

5. The "universal purpose of created things" is a principle stating that the fruit of the earth is God's gift to the entire human family, and that we ought to work so that all are able to benefit from the bounty of the earth and human creativity.

6. The "option for the poor" must be part of dealing with the environmental crisis so that developing nations do not bear the heaviest burdens.

7. Economic and technological development must be "authentic," not just a "mere accumulation of goods and services," according to Pope John Paul II. Authentic development balances respect for nature with human progress and sees human destiny as more than consumption of the goods of the earth.

8. Finally, the relationship between consumption and human population needs to be carefully examined. Although "consumption in developed nations remains the single greatest source of global environmental destruction," the U.S. bishops have noted that "advantaged groups often seem more intent on curbing Third-World births than on restraining the even more voracious consumerism of the developed world" (*Renewing the Earth,*

p. 9). Catholic social teaching urges the promotion of responsible parenthood, rather than coercive population control, in those societies burdened by overpopulation.

A distinctive feature of a Christian concern for the natural environment is its motivation in gratitude rather than in fear. Certainly, ecological catastrophes are frightening to contemplate, and urgent action is needed to correct the imbalances our civilization has created. But if fear alone motivates us, we will only stop our harmful activities. Instead, we need to safeguard the environment and at the same time expand social and economic development to include all people.

Many scientists and commentators doubt that it is possible to both preserve the earth and keep expanding productivity. It may well be that our definition of "progress" will undergo profound changes. The United States, for example, is a civilization dependent on the automobile. What kind of society would we create if we had to rely on mass transit to get around? As Christians, we hope that any changes result from a moral vision as well as from necessity.

Practical Steps

We can become more aware of our responsibilities toward the earth by looking at some practical ways to care for the world. The United Nations Environment Programme produced the "Environmental Sabbath" program in 1989 to draw the attention of people of faith to our urgent ecological problems. The program packet included a Personal Action Guide for the Earth, which outlined practical suggestions for the following areas:

1. Energy: Because burning fossil fuels not only uses up a nonrenewable energy source but also contributes to the

buildup of dangerous gases, the efficient use of energy is crucial. Keeping our automobiles well tuned, using public transportation, insulating our houses, and turning the thermostat a few degrees to reduce our energy use can make an important difference in the way we look at the gift of energy as well as in the future of this important resource.

2. Food: Production of our food has a direct effect on the future of the soil. Some pesticides and fertilizers, while they may in the short run increase agricultural yields, are toxic to the soil over long periods. Raising animals for food is inefficient: the grain they eat could be used to feed humans. In parts of Latin America, the rain forest is being destroyed to provide grazing land for cattle. Reducing one's consumption of meat and supporting laws that ban harmful pesticides can result in greater personal health as well as a better environment.

3. Water: Industrial and agricultural pollution as well as overuse endangers this precious resource. Much household use of water can be reduced by filling washing machines and dishwashers before using them; not running the water while shaving, brushing teeth, and so on; and landscaping with native or drought-resistant plants. Using biodegradable soaps and detergents avoids polluting the ground water.

4. Household toxins and pollutants: Chloroflourocarbons (CFCs), found in some refrigerants, air conditioners, and plastic foam insulation, reduce the protective ozone layer when they are released into the atmosphere. Avoiding Styrofoam products and carefully disposing of refrigerants will help to control CFC pollution.

5. Recycling: By reducing waste through informed con-

sumption and recycling, we can slow down the rate at
which landfills are being used up. Many communities
have made recycling mandatory simply because they
are running out of landfill space.

None of these suggestions is new, and each of them demands
an extra effort on our part to make a small difference in a world
filled with large problems. Small steps may not be "enough" in
the sense that environmental problems need national if not global solutions. But small gestures express our reverence for the
gift of creation. Reverently, we can then support public policy
designed to preserve and enhance the environment.

For Further Discussion

1. Learn about the environmental issues specific to your area
and ask what is being done about them.

2. The U.S. bishops have urged that land ownership not be
concentrated in the hands of a few, but that land be held by as
many people as possible. Believing that the best land stewardship and food production come with "family farms," the bishops have urged the government to assist small-scale farmers.
Should specific laws be enacted to limit the amount of land an
individual or a corporation can hold?

3. The natural world, according to Christian teaching, reflects
the hand of the Creator. Reflect and pray in gratitude about that
part of nature that is your body and your immediate surround-
ings. Ask yourself: how is God evident in that physical reality?

4. Pope John Paul II does not believe that the market alone
can safeguard natural and human environments, but that government must have a role. Are government regulations a necessary restraint on destructive tendencies, or are they a needless
burden on economic productivity?

CHAPTER 7

THE WORLD OF WORK AND THE WORK OF THE WORLD

———

"Every perspective on economic life that is human, moral, and Christian must be shaped by three questions: What does the economy do *for* people? What does it do *to* people? And how do people *participate* in it?" With these words, the U.S. Catholic bishops began their 1986 pastoral letter *Economic Justice for All: Pastoral Letter on Catholic Social Teaching and the U.S. Economy.* This important letter, discussed in chapter 3, addresses the moral implications of economic life. In summary, the bishops insisted that economic decisions and activity have a moral dimension because they affect the human person, either enhancing or diminishing human dignity in the process.

Chapter 3 of this book examines the harmful effects of not participating in the economic life of our nation. An economic system, however, also has moral consequences for those who do participate, who are employed and able to support themselves. This chapter focuses on the importance of work for individuals and for various social institutions.

In *Economic Justice for All*, the bishops referred to the importance of work in several ways: "Work with adequate pay for all who seek it is the primary means for achieving basic justice in our society" (#73); "it is primarily through their daily labor that people make their most important contributions to economic justice" (#96); and "full employment is the foundation of a just economy" (#136).

On the one hand, all of us can readily appreciate the importance of a job. "It is a deep conviction of American culture that work is central to the freedom and well-being of people" (*Economic Justice for All*, #141). On the other hand, work is quite commonly considered a "necessary evil," something we're forced to do so that we can have the money to do what we really want. In such a view, the main purpose of a job is to make as much money as possible.

Work and Modern Social Teaching

Church teaching offers a far richer appraisal of the meaning and potential value of work for humanity. The first of the modern social-teaching encyclicals, *On the Condition of Workers* by Pope Leo XIII, addressed the problems created by the transition to an industrial economy. Today we take industrial and technological development for granted, but a century ago an unprecedented change was taking place: a steadily growing percentage of people were being born and raised in an urban environment. Society no longer seemed a stable, orderly system in which children could expect to live pretty much the same kinds of lives as their parents.

Pope Leo affirmed the dignity of workers and their right to organize into unions and bargain collectively, and the Church also firmly upheld a person's rights to a fair profit and private property. Social transformation has accelerated many times over since his days, to the point that we take change itself for granted. But the "social question" remains the same: if society is indeed changing, what can we do to make it a better place?

Modern ideologies such as communism and capitalism propose their own answers to the social question, but the Church avoids marking out a specific social, economic, or political path for nations to follow. Instead, Catholic teaching has tried to support human dignity and to interpret social change in the light of human dignity and destiny.

A Key to the Social Question

Pope John Paul II has called work "a key, probably the essential key, to the whole social question" (*On Human Work*, #3). In his 1981 encyclical *On Human Work*, the pope not only reaffirmed the Church's traditional support for unions and for a just wage, he explored anew the significance of work in human life. "Man's life is built up every day from work, from work it derives its specific dignity, but at the same time work contains the unceasing measure of human toil and suffering and also of the harm and injustice which penetrate deeply into social life within nations and on the international level" (*On Human Work*, #1). The world of work needs our attention because it can be either a way to build up the human person or a way to destroy it.

For Pope John Paul II, *work* covers a broad range of endeavors: it can be manual or intellectual labor, management or financial activity, paid or unpaid services. The raising of children constitutes work just as surely as toiling on an assembly line or writing a novel. The pope finds in the Book of Genesis evidence that "work is a fundamental dimension of human existence on earth," for God told the first humans to "'be fruitful and multiply, and fill the earth and subdue it'" (Genesis 1:28). "Man [humankind] is the image of God partly through the mandate received from his [their] creator to subdue, to dominate, the earth," wrote the pope. "In carrying out this mandate, man [humanity], every human being, reflects the very action of the creator of the universe" (*On Human Work*, #4).

The Dignity of Work

This creative aspect of work—even work that appears "mechanical" or simply "manual"—makes human labor altogether different from the work of draft animals or machinery. Pope John Paul II insisted that the human person is always "the subject of work," in that work derives its meaning and value by the fact that a human being is doing it. "However true it may be that man is [people are] destined for work and called to it, in the first place work is 'for man [people]' and not man [people] 'for work'" (*On Human Work*, #6).

The central place of the human person in the world of work means that human labor can never be thought of as merely another component of the production process, equal in importance to capital, technology, raw materials, and the like. Labor is not simply something one "sells" in the marketplace like other commodities. The pope condemned what he called "economism," or the way of thinking that reduces labor to an impersonal factor of production. While rejecting Marxist notions of inevitable class conflict and materialism, the pope insisted on the "priority of labor" in the production process. Even capital itself, he pointed out, cannot be created without human labor.

Just as labor is more than just another part of production, so work is more than a necessary evil. "Work is a good thing for man [humankind]—a good thing for his [their] humanity—

because through work man [a person] not only transforms nature, adapting it to his [or her] own needs, but he [or she] also achieves fulfillment as a human being and indeed in a sense becomes 'more a human being'" (*On Human Work*, #9). Although exploitation or slavery can make labor degrading, the pope maintained that work can be ennobling if it is protective and nourishing.

Work in Society

The U.S. Catholic bishops drew heavily from Pope John Paul II's perspective on work in their pastoral letter *Economic Justice for All*. "All work has a threefold moral significance. First, it is a principal way that people exercise the distinctive human capacity for self-expression and self-realization. Second, it is the ordinary way for human beings to fulfill their material needs. Finally, work enables people to contribute to the well-being of the larger community. Work is not only for one's self. It is for one's family, for the nation, and indeed for the benefit of the entire human family" (*Economic Justice for All*, #97).

The U.S. Catholic bishops have recognized that the health of the family, the basic unit of society, depends on productive employment and the payment of a just wage. But work also has significance for "the entire human family." Thus, when choosing a career, young people need to consider not only their personal inclinations and interests, but the effect their work will have on the world as a whole. This broad perspective on the importance of labor is one of the most important contributions the Church can make to the economic life of our nation.

Specific Rights and Duties

The U.S. bishops addressed three specific groups "whose work for justice will be particularly important to the future of the United States economy": working people and labor unions, owners and managers, and citizens and government (*Economic Justice for All,* #101).

Working People and Labor Unions

The bishops reiterated that all who are able to work are obliged to do so. At the same time, people have a right to employment and to just payment for their labor, and it is the duty of society as a whole to respect these rights. "The dignity of workers also requires adequate health care, security for old age or disability, unemployment compensation, healthful working conditions, weekly rest, periodic holidays for recreation and leisure, and reasonable security against arbitrary dismissal," wrote the bishops. "These provisions are all essential if workers are to be treated as persons rather than as a 'factor of production'" (*Economic Justice for All,* #103).

Labor unions, the bishops made clear, have the right to organize and to strike if necessary as well as an obligation to the members and to society as a whole. Workers are encouraged to use their collective power to contribute to the common good of society, particularly in a changing society in which labor needs to adapt quickly to new forms of employment.

Owners and Managers

The bishops gave clear support to the right to private property and to the freedom of entrepreneurship, business, and finance, but they insisted that these be accountable "to the common good and the norms of justice" (*Economic Justice for All,* #110). "Persons in management face many hard choices each day, choices on which the well-being of many others depends," wrote the bishops. "Commitment to the public good and not simply the private good of their firms is at the heart of what it means to call their work a vocation and not simply a career or a job" (#111).

The bishops did not explain how owners and managers are to be held accountable to society for the resources they hold in trust. While they have not advocated state control of business activity, neither do they believe that "a free market automatically produces justice" (#115). Instead, owners and managers are called to recognize their responsibility to make decisions in light of the common good.

Citizens and Government

In the formation of public policy, the government, said the bishops, has a positive role to play. "Society as a whole and in all its diversity is responsible for building up the common good. But it is government's role to guarantee the minimum conditions that make this rich social activity possible, namely, human rights and justice" (*Economic Justice for All*, #122). The bishops quite clearly called for public policies that would ensure jobs to all who are able to work, as well as providing healthcare, retirement benefits, housing, and education. Realizing that such a package is not very popular these days, the bishops hoped their pastoral letter would contribute to a discussion that will build agreement on these fundamental human rights.

Toward a Just Employment Policy

Given how important work is to both the individual and society, it is little wonder that the bishops maintained that "full employment is the foundation of a just society" (*Economic Justice for All*, #136). When workers are left out because of shifts in production, society suffers. As the bishops wrote, "The severe human costs of high unemployment levels become vividly clear when we examine the impact of joblessness on human lives and human dignity....The unemployed often come to feel they are worthless and without a productive role in society" (#141).

Of particular concern to the bishops was the effect of joblessness on the family. "Unemployment takes a terrible toll on the health and stability of both individuals and families. It gives rise to family quarrels, greater consumption of alcohol, child abuse, spouse abuse, divorce, and higher rates of infant mortality" (#141).

According to the recent study *The Truly Disadvantaged,* by University of Chicago sociologist William Julius Wilson, employment is a key factor in when and whether young people decide to marry and form households. While there are certainly a great many influences on family life, economic realities must be considered in any program to strengthen and support this crucial social institution.

The bishops recognized the tremendous social costs brought about by unemployment: family life is undermined; the unemployed pay no taxes but use public services; crime rates rise; and so on. "We cannot afford the economic costs, the social dislocation, and the enormous human tragedies caused by unemployment. In the end, however, what we can least afford is the assault on human dignity that occurs when millions are left without adequate employment" (*Economic Justice for All,* #143).

To address the problem of unemployment, the bishops urged that public policies be designed to reach full employment through monetary and fiscal as well as targeted-employment programs. Private and public job creation was also recommended. Since the bishops wrote their letter, unemployment rates have dropped as the economy has expanded. Yet for non-white people in the inner cities or in many rural areas, unemployment is still unacceptably high. *Economic Justice for All* is a challenge to keep expanding our economy so that members of the so-called "underclass" might also realize their right to a job.

What Is an Economy For?

Economic Justice for All makes recommendations not only on employment but on agriculture, poverty, and international economic relations as well. These recommendations are practical judgments about how best to promote the common good and human dignity through our economic decisions. Agriculture, for example, makes an obvious contribution to the common good in the production of food. But, the bishops emphasized, food production also creates a way of life for human beings, and the organization of agricultural labor and property ownership can either reinforce or threaten democratic institutions. The common good, in the judgment of the bishops, is best served by public policies that encourage moderate-sized family farms rather than concentrated land ownership.

For similar reasons, the bishops urged support of worker-owned businesses and increased cooperation between workers, management, and the owners of capital. Innovative forms of economic activity, said the bishops, should be part of a "new American experiment" in which all sectors of society recognize their responsibility to promote the common good.

Hard Choices Remain

Numerous difficult economic decisions are made every day in the realms of public policy and private enterprise. A classic economic decision involves the choice between inflation and unemployment, both of which have negative consequences.

Economists believe that, generally speaking, low unemployment rates are thought to "trade off" with high inflation rates. One means of controlling inflation is to establish policies that tend to increase unemployment. To the extent that this is so, policymakers have to chose between the two evils of inflation and unemployment. Which do we prefer?

Other choices must also be made. High cost is often cited as an argument against employment-training programs, yet our military budget is tremendously expensive. Nor does military spending generate as much expansion in the economy as does nonmilitary spending. How much are we willing to spend for security? For a more just economy?

Catholic social teaching has no specific answers for these questions. Instead, the Church asks us to evaluate our economy on the basis of its support of the common good and the dignity of the individual. *Economic Justice for All* and *On Human Work* encourage us to seek the deepest meaning in human economic activity and to search for the structures and decisions that will best serve human beings. Our tradition may not offer easy answers to difficult problems, but it does offer hope. "No utopia is possible on this earth; but as believers in the redemptive love of God and as those who have experienced God's forgiving mercy," wrote the bishops, "we know that God's providence is not and will not be lacking to us today" (*Economic Justice for All*, #364).

For Further Discussion

1. Pope John Paul II has said that work has its meaning and value because the worker is a human being. Does this make sense to you? How is work done by an animal or a machine different from the same work done by a human?

2. Make and compare two lists. First, give all the reasons

why you do the work you do. Second, list all the things you would like to work for. Are there any ways you can make the first list more like the second?

3. The choice of a career is one of the most important decisions a person can make. What key considerations ought to be included in the process of making that decision?

CHAPTER 8

HUMAN SOLIDARITY

———

At the end of a book on social justice, one can easily feel overwhelmed by the number and difficulty of problems to which our faith calls us to respond. A good antidote to that feeling is the perspective of Pope John Paul II, especially as expressed in two encyclical letters, *On Social Concern* and *On the Hundredth Anniversary of* Rerum Novarum. These documents address the work of international development from the perspective of faith in Jesus Christ as Redeemer. This is a wide perspective indeed: the pope has insisted that our faith obliges us to address not simply one social issue or the economy of a single country, but to work for a better life for every human being in the whole world. The good news is that the pope has offered hope and a vision of a better world that is not only attractive, it is possible.

He has stated our responsibility in the clearest terms: "Anyone wishing to renounce the *difficult yet noble task* of improving the lot of man [humankind] in his [their] totality, and of all people, with the excuse that the struggle is difficult and that constant effort is required, or simply because of the experience of defeat and the need to begin again, that person would be betraying the will of God the Creator" (*On Social Concern*, #30). The pope has suggested that we make a serious study of the stewardship parable of the Talents (Matthew 25:14–30) and face our duty to work for the full development of every person.

"But," we may ask ourselves, "how can this be? I don't have the power to save the world." And that is correct. *On Social Concern* is primarily a document of faith in the saving power of Jesus Christ, but that very faith leads us not only to face the world around us, but also to embrace the cause of human dignity and freedom. *On Social Concern* is also a practical document that points the way toward change, in our hearts and in our patterns of behavior.

A Tribute to Pope Paul VI

On Social Concern, written on the twentieth anniversary of Pope Paul VI's encyclical *On the Development of Peoples*, reinforces and expands the earlier work. According to Pope John Paul II, the three important contributions of *On the Development of Peoples* are

1. its identifying the development question as a moral issue
2. its viewing the "social question" from an international perspective
3. its drawing a connection between development and peace

Pope Paul VI understood the increasing "interdependence" of the world community: as a result of modern communications, events in one part of the world speedily affect what happens in other parts. For example, a rise in oil prices in the Middle East affects the cost of manufactured goods in the United States; a decision by the U.S. Federal Reserve Board to raise interest rates increases the cost of a water-treatment plant in Africa. Although social and economic interdependence is a fact, it is not matched by political interdependence or some form of effective international governance. The obligation to foster development, then, falls to individuals and individual nations.

Pope John Paul II contended that despite the insights and hopes expressed in *On the Development of Peoples,* the lot of people in the poorest countries has deteriorated in the past twenty years. The gap between the economies of countries in the industrialized North and less developed South is widening, he wrote, and pervasive illiteracy and often a lack of respect for human rights still characterize poor nations. Worst of all, millions of people around the globe suffer daily from inadequate housing, unemployment or underemployment, and inflation resulting from the burden of international debt.

Nevertheless, Pope John Paul II also identified several positive trends in this period. These include a growing awareness of human rights, a deepening acceptance of global interdependence, a greater concern for the environment, and the noteworthy dedication of many individuals to global development. As the pope wrote, such changing attitudes give hope and suggest the possibility of genuine human development. Events were to justify many of his hopes within a few years.

A New International Scene

Writing before the fall of Communism in 1989, Pope John Paul II identified the division of the world into East and West as one of the greatest barriers to international cooperation and mutual assistance. Though a tribute to the work of Pope Leo XIII and those who sought to put his teaching into practice, *On the Hundredth Anniversary of* Rerum Novarum, written after momentous political and social changes altered the international landscape, is also an analysis of the present world situation and a look to the future.

As discussed in chapter 7, Pope Leo XIII supported the rights of private property and condemned class warfare as a means of social progress, but he also defended the rights of workers to organize and to be paid a just wage. He believed that socialism would hurt the laborer by taking away private property and distorting the functions of the state.

Pope John Paul II asserted that "the fundamental error of socialism is anthropological in nature. Socialism considers the individual person simply as an element, a molecule within the social organism, so that the good of the individual is completely subordinated to the functioning of the socio-economic mechanism" (*On the Hundredth Anniversary,* #13). The state controls more and more social functions, actually making it harder for the individual to realize his or her true identity.

The pope identified the root problem as atheism, for "it is by responding to the call of God contained in the being of things that man [humankind] becomes aware of his [their] transcendent dignity. Every individual must give this response, which constitutes the apex of his [or her] humanity, and no social mechanism or collective subject can substitute for it" (*On the Hundredth Anniversary,* #13). The role of the Church's social teaching is, then, to insist upon the fundamental truths of human life as a basis for a just society.

The Fall of Communism

In fact, the role of the Church in the fall of the Soviet bloc was crucial. Pope John Paul II asserted that in the social and political transitions of 1989 "an important, even decisive, contribution was made by *the Church's commitment to defend and promote human rights*" (*On the Hundredth Anniversary,* #22). Furthermore, "the events of 1989 are an example of the success of willingness to negotiate and of the Gospel spirit in the face of an adversary determined not to be bound by moral principles....In a certain sense, it was a struggle born of prayer, and it would have been unthinkable without immense trust in God, the Lord of history, who carries the human heart in his hands" (*On the Hundredth Anniversary,* #25).

Although the pope used the term "socialism" in this particular instance, he has also used "Communism" with a capital C or "Real Socialism" in quotes to suggest a particular incarnation of an ideal—the Soviet-style Marxist-Leninist tradition—rather than the ideal itself. A better general term would be "Communism."

The pope recognized that the other key factor in the breakdown of Communism was its internal economic collapse, but that in itself was a "consequence of the violation of human rights to private initiative, to ownership of property and to freedom in the economic sector. To this must be added the cultural and national dimension: it is not possible to understand the human person on the basis of economics alone, nor to define the person simply on the basis of class membership" (*On the Hundredth Anniversary,* #24).

As a staunch critic of Communism, the pope might be expected to advocate capitalism as a model for economic development. In *On the Hundredth Anniversary of* Rerum Novarum, he noted that the question is complex, depending in part on how one defines *capitalism*. He wrote that he supports an economic system promoting "the fundamental and positive role of business, the market, private property" and "free human creativity in the economic sector." At the same time, the legal framework binding such a system must serve "human freedom in its totality" (*On the Hundredth Anniversary,* #42). Human freedom, obedient to a transcendent truth, is essential to the full realization of human dignity.

As encouraged as he was by the dissolution of the Soviet bloc, the pope recognized that progress would not be automatic. "Vast multitudes are still living in conditions of great material and moral poverty. The collapse of the Communist system in so many countries certainly removes an obstacle to facing these problems in an appropriate and realistic way, but it is not enough to bring about their solution. Indeed, there is a risk that a radical capitalist ideology could spread which refuses even to consider these problems, in the *a priori* belief that any attempt to solve them is doomed to failure, and which blindly entrusts their solution to the free development of market forces" (*On the Hundredth Anniversary,* #42).

Although Pope John Paul II pointed out the weakness in socialist theory, he also made it clear that the defeat of "Real Socialism" as practiced in the Soviet Union did not "leave capitalism as the only model of economic organization." Instead, he criticized features of capitalism that he has seen as harmful to the human person. By the same token, he has supported social and economic developments that foster freedom and creativity, carefully limiting and qualifying his analysis so as not to appear to give support to a specific ideology.

Perhaps the following quote from *On the Hundredth Anniversary* explains his reasoning: "The Church has no models to present; models that are real and truly effective can only arise within the framework of different historical situations, through the efforts of all those who responsibly confront concrete problems in all their social, economic, political and cultural aspects, as these interact with one another. For such a task the Church offers her social teaching as an *indispensable and ideal orientation*, a teaching which, as already mentioned, recognizes the positive value of the market and of enterprise, but which at the same time points out that these need to be oriented toward the common good" (#43). Rather than being opposed or in favor of social systems, the pope wants to affirm the good and criticize the bad in all of them.

True Development: A Christian Vision

Side by side with the miseries of underdevelopment is the problem of what Pope John Paul II called "superdevelopment": the *"excessive* availability of every kind of material goods for the benefit of certain social groups" which "easily makes people slaves of 'possession' and of immediate gratification.... All of us experience firsthand the sad effects of this blind submission to pure consumerism: in the first place a crass materialism, and at the same time a *radical dissatisfaction,* because one quickly learns—unless one is shielded from the flood of publicity and the ceaseless and tempting offers of products—that the more one possesses the more one wants, while deeper aspirations remain unsatisfied and perhaps even stifled" (*On Social Concern*, #28).

True development is not simply a matter of material goods. Development must include "the *cultural, transcendent and religious dimensions* of man [people] and society" or it will end by enslaving us further (*On Social Concern,* #46). Respect for human rights and for the cultural integrity of minorities, collaboration with others, and care of the environment are all characteristic of genuine human development.

We in the United States may become uncomfortable whenever concepts like "superdevelopment" and "consumerism" are mentioned. It is important to note that the pope has not suggested there is anything wrong with things themselves or with technological and material progress. "The danger of the misuse of material goods and the appearance of artificial needs should in no way hinder the regard we have for the new goods and resources placed at out disposal and the use we make of them. On the contrary, we must see them as a gift from God and as a response to the human vocation, which is fully realized in Christ" (*On Social Concern,* #29). It is what we do with the things we have that is important.

Is International Development Realistic?

"Just as there is a collective responsibility for avoiding war," wrote Pope John Paul II, "so too there is a collective responsibility for promoting development" (*On the Hundredth Anniversary,* #52). Nations must join together to intervene in ways that foster "trust in the human potential of the poor, and consequently in their ability to make a positive contribution to economic prosperity. But to accomplish this, the poor be they individuals or nations need to be provided with realistic opportunities" (#52). That will require "sacrificing the positions of income and power enjoyed by the more developed countries" (#52).

The Church is confident that authentic economic liberation is possible, for two basic reasons: first, Christ has promised us the kingdom; second, through Christ, each person becomes capable of bringing the Holy Spirit's action into the world. This view does not deny the difficulty of the struggle. "The path [of development] is *long and complex*," wrote Pope John Paul II, "and what is more it is constantly threatened because of the intrinsic frailty of human resolutions and achievements, and because of the *mutability* of very unpredictable external circumstances. Nevertheless, one must have the courage to set out on this path, and, where some steps have been taken or a part of the journey made, the courage to go on to the end" (*On Social Concern*, #38).

Finding the courage for such a journey is tough because it challenges our faith: our world demands results, values "the bottom line," and scoffs at anything but hardheaded logic. But as people of faith, we believe in the resurrection of the dead and the redemption of humankind through the blood of the Cross. Part of living out and nurturing our life of faith is to keep on trying to build a more compassionate way of relating to one another.

Christian hope extends beyond immediate results and momentary conditions. "We can say therefore—as we struggle amidst the obscurities and deficiencies of *underdevelopment* and *superdevelopment*—that one day this corruptible body will put on incorruptibility, this mortal body immortality (cf. *1 Cor* 15:54), when the Lord 'delivers the Kingdom to God the Father' (v. 24) and all the works and actions that are worthy of man [humankind] will be redeemed" (*On Social Concern*, #31). Such a tremendous vision does not mean we can ignore practical results or prudential counsel, but it does reflect the eternal perspective to which Christians are called.

The Church can be wrong in its specific, historically conditioned social judgments. So can any one of us. But we cannot get discouraged and give up. Christ has set us free to love God and our neighbor and will use even the most modest of our achievements and intentions to build his kingdom.

Conversion and Solidarity

Seeking "greater justice" or building a "more just society" is a continual process much like that of conversion itself. In the international world order, conversion shows forth in the virtue of solidarity, the moral and social attitude that accompanies the recognition of global interdependence.

"[Solidarity] is not a feeling of vague compassion or shallow distress at the misfortunes of so many people near and far," wrote Pope John Paul II. "On the contrary, it is *a firm and persevering determination* to commit oneself to the *common good*; that is to say to the good of all and of each individual, because we are *all* really responsible *for all*" (*On Social Concern*, #38). Instead of exploiting others for profit and then making token donations to organizations that feed or clothe the poor, we can act in solidarity with them by helping them to participate in and share with us the benefits of society.

Ultimately, solidarity is linked to love for others, especially for the poor. "Justice will never be fully attained," the pope has said, "unless people see in the poor person, who is asking help in order to survive, not an annoyance or a burden, but an opportunity for showing kindness and a chance for greater enrichment. Only such an awareness can give the courage needed to face the risk and the change involved in every authentic attempt to come to the aid of another" (*On the Hundredth Anniversary*, #58.)

For Pope John Paul II, solidarity is essential for achieving an authentic international order: "For world peace is inconceivable unless the world's leaders come to recognize that *interdependence* in itself demands the abandonment of the politics of blocs, the sacrifice of all forms of economic, military or political imperialism, and the transformation of mutual distrust into *collaboration*" (*On Social Concern*, #39).

Solidarity in Practice

In the concluding section of this great encyclical letter, the pope appealed to all his readers. "I wish to ask them to be convinced of the seriousness of the present moment and of each one's individual responsibility, and to implement—by the way they live as individuals and as families, by the use of their resources, by their civic activity, by contributing to economic and political decisions and by personal commitment to national and international undertakings—the *measures* inspired by solidarity and love of preference for the poor" (*On Social Concern*, #47). By such an appeal the pope opened wide the door for us to change our behavior and bring about needed reform.

Each of us must determine how best to bring the virtue of solidarity into our lives. For some, it may be accepting a rigorous life as a missionary or international-development volunteer. For another, praying for famine-ravaged lands might be the best gift of self. Still others may express their concern for our sisters and brothers through a combination of material aid, public-policy advocacy, and prayer.

The U.S. Catholic bishops have chosen a number of different ways to express their solidarity with the poor of other lands. In 1988 they issued *A Word of Solidarity*, which called for the promotion of religious freedom throughout the nations of Eastern Europe and the Soviet Union. In 1986 the administrative board of the U.S. Catholic Conference urged the withdrawal of investment from South Africa to pressure its government to end apartheid.

The U.S. bishops have not directed all their attention to foreign governments. In 1981 they called upon all parties to end military support for the conflicts in Central America. Taking issue with the U.S. government, the bishops' statement argued that internal poverty and the denial of human rights were the root causes of conflict, not Soviet subversion. Since 1981 the bishops have reiterated and elaborated upon that position in congressional testimony.

While at times urging specific measures to build society or support human dignity, "the Church well knows that *no temporal achievement* is to be identified with the Kingdom of God, but that all such achievements simply *reflect* and in a sense *anticipate* the glory of the Kingdom, the Kingdom which we await at the end of history, when the Lord will come again. But that expectation can never be an excuse for lack of concern for people in their concrete personal situations and in their social, national and international life" (*On Social Concern*, #48).

Christian Solidarity and Liberation

"Peoples and individuals aspire to be free: their search for full development signals their desire to overcome the many obstacles preventing them from enjoying a 'more human life'" (*On Social Concern*, #46). This universal desire for freedom unites the peoples of the entire world, those that suffer from a lack of goods as well as those who are surrounded by more than they could ever use. The paths toward final liberation in each case may be different, but all people must overcome "sin and the structures produced by sin," as Pope John Paul II has put it, if they are to be truly free.

The good news about Catholic social teaching is that we can do something and we don't have to do everything. We can neither allow guilt to shut our eyes to human misery around us, nor delude ourselves into thinking we can build an earthly utopia. We can accept ourselves as imperfect creatures and, in the process, learn more about the God whom we worship.

Ours is not a perfect life, to be sure, but a life of grace and possibility. It is a life outlined with the enduring simplicity of the prophet Micah: "What does the LORD require of you but to do justice, and to love kindness, and to walk humbly with your God?" (6:8).

For Further Discussion

1. "Development is the new name for peace," Pope Paul VI wrote in *On the Development of Peoples*. According to the U.S. bishops, much of the strife in Central America is due to the inequitable sharing of the benefits of development and of accumulated social wealth. Take the time to learn a little bit more about Central America. Does the bishops' perspective make sense? What should the United States do?

2. Pope John Paul II has spoken of advertising and the news media creating "artificial needs" in developed countries. Are you aware of artificial needs in your own life? How do you decide what you "really need" and what you only want but can comfortably live without?

3. Because the world is interdependent—that is, what affects one country eventually affects all others—recent Catholic social-teaching documents have urged the formation of some kind of world government to ensure fairness in international relations. Is such a world authority possible? Is it a good idea?

BIBLIOGRAPHY

Church Documents

Papal Documents

Leo XIII. *On the Condition of Workers.* In *Contemporary Catholic Social Teaching.* Washington, D.C.: U.S. Catholic Conference, 1991.

John XXIII. *Peace on Earth.* Washington, D.C.: U.S. Catholic Conference, 1963.

Paul VI. *On the Development of Peoples.* Washington, D.C.: U.S. Catholic Conference, 1967.

John Paul II. *On Human Work.* Washington, D.C.: U.S. Catholic Conference, 1981.

———. *On the Christian Meaning of Human Suffering.* Washington, D.C.: U.S. Catholic Conference, 1984.

———. *On Social Concern.* Washington, D.C.: U.S. Catholic Conference, 1987.

———. *On the Dignity and Vocation of Women.* Washington, D.C.: U.S. Catholic Conference, 1988.

———. *On the Hundredth Anniversary of* Rerum Novarum. Boston: St. Paul Books and Media, 1991.

————. *The Gospel of Life*. Rome, Italy: Libreria Editrice Vaticana, 1995.

U.S. Bishops

72 Midwestern Bishops. *Toward Community in the Heartland: Strangers and Guests*. In *Origins* 10, no. 6 (June 26, 1980).

A Report on "The Challenge of Peace" and Policy Developments, 1983–1988. In *Origins* 18, no. 9 (July 21, 1988).

A Word of Solidarity, A Call for Justice: A Statement on Religious Freedom in Eastern Europe and the Soviet Union. In *Origins* 18, no. 26 (Dec. 8, 1988).

Ad Hoc Committee for a Pastoral Response to Women's Concerns. *One in Christ Jesus: Toward a Pastoral Response to the Concerns of Women for Church and Society*. Washington, D.C.: U.S. Catholic Conference, 1993.

Brothers and Sisters to Us. In *Origins* 9, no. 24 (Nov. 29, 1979).

Committee on Pro-Life Activities. *Guidelines for Legislation on Life-Sustaining Treatment*. In *Origins* 14, no. 32 (Jan. 24, 1985).

Confronting a Culture of Violence. Washington, D.C.: U.S. Catholic Conference, 1994.

Discrimination and Christian Conscience. In *Pastoral Letters of the U.S. Hierarchy*, ed. Hugh J. Nolan. Huntington, Ind.: Our Sunday Visitor, Inc., 1971.

Economic Justice for All: Pastoral Letter on Catholic Social Teaching and the U.S. Economy. Washington, D.C.: U.S. Catholic Conference, 1986.

Heritage and Hope: Evangelization in the United States. In *Origins* 20, no. 26 (Dec. 6, 1990).

Krol, Cardinal John. *SALT II: A Statement of Support*. In *Origins* 9, no. 13 (Sept. 13, 1979).

Pastoral Plan for Pro-Life Activities: A Reaffirmation. In *Origins* 15, no. 24 (Nov. 2, 1985).

Renewing the Earth: An Invitation to Reflection and Action on the Environment in Light of Catholic Social Teaching. Washington, D.C.: U.S. Catholic Conference, 1992.

Statement on Capital Punishment. In *Origins* 10, no. 24 (Nov. 27, 1980).

Statement on National Race Crisis. In *Pastoral Letters of the U.S. Hierarchy,* ed. Hugh J. Nolan. Huntington, Ind.: Our Sunday Visitor, Inc., 1971.

The Challenge of Peace: God's Promise and Our Response. Washington, D.C.: U.S. Catholic Conference, 1983.

The Harvest of Justice Is Sown in Peace. Washington, D.C.: U.S. Catholic Conference, 1994.

Vatican Documents

Catechism of the Catholic Church. Washington, D.C.: U.S. Catholic Conference—Libreria Editrice Vaticana, 1994.

Declaration on Euthanasia. In *Origins* 10, no. 10 (Aug. 14, 1980).

Instruction of Christian Liberation and Freedom. Washington, D.C.: U.S. Catholic Conference, 1986.

Pontifical Council for the Family. *In the Service of Life.* Washington, D.C.: U.S. Catholic Conference, 1992.

Pontifical Justice and Peace Commission. *The Church and Racism.* In *Origins* 18, no. 37 (Feb. 23, 1989).

Sacred Congregation for the Doctrine of the Faith. *Declaration on Abortion.* Washington, D.C.: U.S. Catholic Conference, 1975.

Second Vatican Council. *Pastoral Constitution on the Church in the Modern World.* In *The Documents of Vatican II,* ed. Walter M. Abbott, S.J., and Very Rev. Msgr. Joseph Gallagher. New York: America Press, 1965.

General

Langan, John, S.J. "Capital Punishment in America Today." *Respect Life.* Washington, D.C.: U.S. Catholic Conference, 1986.

Wilson, William Julius. *The Truly Disadvantaged: The Inner City, the Underclass, and Public Policy.* Chicago: University of Chicago Press, 1987.